BECOME AN AWESOME

SOFTWARE
ARCHITECT

BOOK 1

FOUNDATION

2019

ANATOLY VOLKHOVER

BECOME AN AWESOME
SOFTWARE
ARCHITECT

BOOK 1

FOUNDATION

2019

ISBN: 978-1-69727-106-5 (paperback)

In loving memories of Nika, who kept our cave warm and our minds sane for so many years.

TABLE OF CONTENTS

PREFACE

My name is Anatoly. I am a serial entrepreneur and software architect from Silicon Valley, with a background in mathematics, physics and computer science. I am one very lucky dude. I studied at the best math & physics school in the former Soviet Union, which has given me a solid foundation for further technological and scientific advancement. I moved to California in early 1990s and immediately dived into an endless stream of projects of varying complexity, across many generations of computer hardware and software stacks.

I started coding when I was 12, initially working on IBM System/360 mainframes, then moved to DEC PDP and VAX systems in 1980s, then to early PCs running MS DOS and then Windows in early 1990, to Tandem NonStop in late 1990s, web apps in early 2000s, and mobile apps and AWS cloud nowadays. I was crazy enough to never shy away from a challenge. I designed and built distributed object-oriented databases, programming languages, virtual machines, business process automation, banking systems, e-commerce solutions, airline booking engines, social web sites, mobile apps, marketing platforms, games, biometric algorithms, and God knows what else. Just as I said, one lucky dude!

Throughout all this time, I remained hands-on with all my projects and continuously looked for ways to make myself and my teams more efficient in building and maintaining software solutions. The meant a lot of trial and error, lots of coding, thinking, and refactoring. At certain point, I became so efficient that I could build a full-fledged custom enterprise solution all by myself, or with a very small crew.

That's when my wife Elena told me that keeping all this knowledge to myself is criminal. This is how the idea of this book came about.

San Francisco, California
October 2019

CONTACT

I love making new friends. Feel free to connect with me. I welcome any kind of feedback and enjoy meeting like-minded engineers and entrepreneurs. Below are the links to my web site and to my LinkedIn page. Use whichever one is more convenient for you.

My web site

https://anatoly.com

My LinkedIn page

https://linkedin.com/in/anatolyvolkhover

ACKNOWLEDGMENTS

I am forever grateful to Victor Eydus, Wesley Tanaka, Max Kuperman, Ken Hilton, Andris Birkmanis, Arthur Shir and Stanislav Tsvetkov for their insightful feedback on the early draft of the manuscript. The comments I received not only helped making this book more accurate and more digestible, but also created a long list of topics for me to cover in the future publications. Thank you!

A very special thank you to my amazing wife Elena, who is the reason behind me getting into writing in the first place. It was Elena's idea for me to share what I learned over the years, paving way for this book and for a few more to come.

A warm hug to my Dad, who got me hooked on computer programming back in my childhood and created many code tinkering opportunities for me to master the craft early. Thank you, Dad!

Many thanks to all amazing engineers whom I worked with throughout my career, those who provided me with so many mind-boggling puzzles to solve, those who taught me by example, and of course those who invested years of their lives into implementing my designs.

I am also grateful to the engineering team at Minted, for trusting me and my methods, and for providing a continuous stream of inspiration.

– Anatoly Volkhover

INTRODUCTION

In early 2019, a young first-time entrepreneur (let's call him Joe) called me for advice. He had an awesome idea for his new startup. Joe raised some seed capital from his friends and family six months earlier and used most of it on development of the technology that would power his new business. As Joe was rolling the service out into the market, he realized that several changes must be applied to his technology for the business to succeed – hardly a surprise, since most products go through a lot of fine-tuning before they are ready for their prime. Joe wasn't surprised at the need to make changes either. He got surprised by his team though. His engineers estimated the cost of the proposed changes to be extremely high, close to the original investment made into building the entire system. Joe was devastated. He had very little cash left, and it was all earmarked for PR and marketing. Joe called me, crying for help. He hoped that I might be able to find a "smart" way to fix his system on a shoestring budget.

Long story short, there wasn't a smart way. I couldn't help Joe, and not for the lack of trying. His team was correct in their assessment. The new requirements invalidated the principles on which his software was built upon. Essentially, Joe had to rebuild his entire technology from scratch. Needless to say, no investor would give him the $$ to fix his technology without having a solid proof of sales. Joe asked around, looking for either the capital or a technical solution, came out empty handed and, a few months later, folded his business.

This was not the first time when I was asked to save the day and couldn't. I met many entrepreneurs facing the very same challenge. I worked for a number of companies carrying an excessively large and expensive engineering workforce to maintain and extend their existing systems. I saw low engineering velocity slowing a business's ability to innovate to a crawl. My own very first startup caused countless sleepless nights and resulted in devastating personal financial losses, as well as years spent in an attempt to fix the early mistakes.

Anyone with experience in software engineering will readily explain this problem is hardly a new one. They may point you at the stats showing 70% of the software projects fail. They may also tell you of numerous books containing well-explained remedies, from reusable software design patterns to coding style guides. Yet, despite all the advice that's out there, the projects still fail in scores, and we are still surrounded by poorly constructed software – the software that companies cannot improve, because every time they try, everything falls apart. And as complexity of the software grows, the problem gets worse.

What differentiates the failed projects from the successful ones? *All successful projects had better architecture – and better architecture comes from better software architects.*

Great architects aren't born. They are a product of decades of building real-life solutions and relentless learning. They become really good at their trade closer to the retirement age. But most startups are fostered by young entrepreneurs who dare to try but lack the experience. They also lack the $$ to hire a silver-haired architect to join their team from day one. Left to their own faculties, the entrepreneurs and their engineering teams quickly get on the path of learning from their own mistakes. Eventually they discover this is the most expensive way of learning. Over time they get better, and some become the true masters of the craft – but way too late to make a difference for their early-day projects.

This book is meant to break the vicious circle. It isn't a textbook, at least not in the traditional sense. It is a business-centric practical guide to software architecture, intended for software engineers, technology executives, students of computer science, and tech-savvy entrepreneurs who want to de-risk their entrepreneurial endeavors or to fast-track their careers in software engineering. I have personally battle-tested every single recipe from this book. The recipes are highly practical, reflect 30 years of my experience in the field, and are current for building mid- to large-scale systems in 2019.

Enjoy, and Godspeed!

HOW TO READ THIS BOOK

The book is intended to be consumed sequentially, from the very beginning to the very end. The sequence is important, since the recipes in the book are somewhat interdependent. When new terminology is introduced, I explain it at the first encounter only.

I wanted the book to be concise, so I had to curb my enthusiasm of going down each rabbit hole and explaining everything. I assume that the reader knows how to write code and understands the mainstream software engineering jargon. If you encounter a term which you haven't heard of, or are only vaguely familiar with, I encourage you to look it up and discover its true meaning, before continuing.

You should let your preconceptions go while reading this book. Forget what you learned in school, and how you do your work today. Try to be as open-minded as you can. Some of the concepts and recommendations may appear foreign or far-fetched to you – and I suggest you pay very close attention to those; that's where you get most of the value. I did not write this book to make you comfortable. I wrote it specifically to confront the inefficient way the software is created today, and to show you the awesome alternatives, proven effective by many years and many projects.

Code examples in the book are all in TypeScript, unless specified otherwise. I picked TypeScript for several reasons: (a) it is an extension of universally understood JavaScript, (b) it has most of the features of the more established enterprise-grade programming languages while remaining readable and concise, (c) because I like it a lot, and had great success using it in projects of varying scale and complexity. If you are not familiar with TypeScript, you should be able to understand the examples nevertheless – but of course I do encourage you to check out the documentation posted on *https://www.typescriptlang.org* which is an excellent source for learning the language. Code snippets are abbreviated to make them more readable. I do not expect you to compile or run them; simply read and make sure you understand them. Code snippets are easy to spot; they look like this:

```
<code>
console.log( `Hello, World!` );
</code>
```

When a program's output is included, it looks like this:

```
<output>
  Hello, World!
</output>
```

I did my best to pack as much advice on every page of the book as possible, to the point where almost every sentence is there for a reason. Please take your time. Take it slowly, one chapter at a time. Spend the time to fully understand the diagrams and the code samples; they are key to full comprehension of the concepts outlined in the book.

Some chapters ended up covering more ground than you may find comfortable to consume at once. In those, I strategically placed *breakpoints*. They look like this:

Contrary to the common meaning (an instruction to pause the program for debugging purposes), breakpoints in this book mean something entirely different: they are suggesting you to *take a break and get some rest*.

I incorporated a few other hints into the body of the book. The most critical pieces of advice look like this:

<important>
Weather forecast for tonight: dark. (George Carlin)
</important>

At the end of each chapter, you will find a brief summary, and a link to discuss the chapter's material online. Summaries are easy to spot; they look like this:

If you can't beat them, arrange to have them beaten. (George Carlin)

https://anatoly.com/welcome

Ready to start turning pages?

WHAT IS SOFTWARE ARCHITECTURE?

Some people have no idea what they're doing, and a lot of them are really good at it.
        – George Carlin

If someone asks you this question – *"What is software architecture?"* – how would you answer? Why can't you just sit down and start writing code to implement your idea? Or can you? Why would anyone invest the time, money, and effort into creating a bunch of diagrams and documents?

Just for curiosity's sake, I asked the engineers on my team.

"Hey guys," I said after we wrapped up one of the meetings. "If I ask you to define the term *software architecture* for me, how would you do this?"

One of the engineers (let's call him Tom), said quickly:

"Architecture is a process of *creating a structure* for a software project". Tom looked around the room as if he just earned a free lunch.

"Well…" I said, "Why do you need to create a structure for your project?"

That got him thinking.

"I guess to create a plan, break down the project into tasks…" Tom was no longer certain about that free lunch.

"To review the plan and ensure it is solid," another engineer suggested.

"To ensure flexibility of the solution," another suggestion came up.

I pressed on:

"Why do you need a plan? What are the tasks for? Why review the plan? Why is flexibility important?"

It took another 15 minutes of digging until we got somewhere:

"To improve velocity of development"

"To reduce costs"

"To make software maintainable"

What do you think? What is software architecture, and what is its purpose?

<important>

Software architecture is a series of decisions intended to reduce the cost of building and changing your software.

</important>

Think about it. When you are building a software solution, it is usually intended to address a business need. The more time you spend building it, the higher engineering costs you will incur. The longer your time-to-market, the higher the business risks and the costs of lost opportunities will be. Once your solution is built and deployed, your business will likely face the need to extend or change the software further, to optimize your sales funnels, to expand the addressable market segment, to continue innovating, and to adjust for ever-changing market and legal conditions. Such changes go far beyond the original plan for the system and are almost impossible to predict. You will be facing the challenge of changing your system in ways you never anticipated. But despite the unknowns, there are certain principles of software construction which help reduce the cost of the planned software development, as well as minimize the negative impact of the future changes. Such principles, once applied to a particular application, are usually referred to as *software architecture*.

The most impactful principles are outlined in this book. Optimally, the investment into creation of software architecture is made upfront, before a single line of code is written, and before the development team is hired. Your architecture will define your hiring needs. Then, expect a relatively small investment into maintaining the architecture throughout the life of your system.

Almost every software engineer knows that having an architecture is important. Not everyone understands the reasons for having it. Remember the reason we need an architecture in the first place: *reducing the cost of building and changing your software over time*. This alone will help you make good intuitive decisions in many cases.

Now that we established the reason for creating an architecture, the next question is – how do we approach it? Which decisions we must make to cover everything of importance?

It's time to take the first step into your awesomeness: The Architect's Hit List.

<tldr>

The main purpose of software architecture is to reduce the cost of building and changing the software.

https://anatoly.com/software-architecture

</tldr>

CHAPTER 1
THE ARCHITECT'S HIT LIST

Scratch any cynic and you will find a disappointed idealist.
– George Carlin

Back in 2004, I worked as a consultant for a large tour operator. The company had an ambitious plan for replacing their legacy system with a completely new solution, using the latest and greatest in software architecture and hardware.

Travel products tend to grow very complex, due to the large variety of options, insanely non-standard vendor contracts, the high number of packaging variants, and pricing that changes daily to maximize the revenue based on availability, demand, seasonality, and multitude of other factors.

The company spent 10 months gathering the requirements for their new system, which was supposed to sell any travel product under the sun, never mind the complexity. Once the requirements were gathered, they submitted them to the architecture team for recommendations and estimates. The process took another 3 months, after which the approach was committed to paper, and time and cost estimates were submitted for approval. The projected cost was in 8 digits, and the time was estimated at 2 years, for a team of 30 experienced engineers.

I was not directly involved with the project and left to pursue my entrepreneurial endeavors soon after it started. I've heard on the grapevine that the company spent eight (8!) years and 6x of the initial $$ estimate. Eight years is an eternity in technology world. Everything conceived 8 years back is considered terribly outdated, even if fully functional. A ludicrous amount of cash and 240 years of human lives were sacrificed on the project's altar, only to produce a system that was outdated upon arrival.

Throughout my career, I saw similar failures (or extremely expensive successes), on various scales, way too often to call them accidental. There is a flaw in the process, which plagues the majority of technology projects nowadays.

To explain it better, let's take a short detour and look outside of the all-familiar software engineering domain. Let's consider what *automakers* are doing.

Think of what it takes to build a car. The car should meet the drivability requirements, such as maximum speed, fuel consumption, handling, acceleration, safety, etc. But this is only a tip of the iceberg, as the engineering work for cars goes much further. First, the car should be *maintainable by third parties*, such as independent mechanics and dealerships. Second, it should be easy to *swap replacement parts* by independent body shops. Third, the car should be *quick and inexpensive to assemble*, which is achieved through proper architecture of the *assembly line*. Fourth, the assembly line must ensure *consistent quality*, largely achieved by the processes and equipment which *eliminate or limit human errors and make the errors easily detectable* before the car leaves the factory. Fifth, the assembly lines are designed to quickly switch from one car model to another, allowing the automaker to *quickly respond to the market's demand.*

No surprises there, right? Then why aren't we thinking the same way about software? For some reason, many of us think that collecting the functional requirements for a software product or service and building a system around those requirements is all it takes. But then – drawing a parallel with an automaker – we build a car that is drivable, but the kind of car that is tedious and expensive to produce, impossible to fix, and which next-generation model would have to be redesigned from scratch. Then we suffer for years, seeing how our ability to innovate and adapt slows down to a crawl. Teams and managers change, and finally someone proposes a radical fix – a "rewrite". A few more years, and the new management makes a daring decision to put an end to the pain and suffering and approves the "rewrite" budget. The engineers get all excited at the opportunity to fix everything that went wrong, and they take off on the crusade of re-architecting everything… only to make the same mistakes all over again. They create a new, expanded functional spec, and they leave the non-functional requirements out. The vicious circle continuous… unless the business dies and puts an end to everyone's misery.

This cycle is so commonplace that I met scores of young developers who never saw anything but this wasteful and reckless way of building technology, which makes it the new norm.

This is exactly what happened to the tour operator I worked for. They invested into collecting the *functional requirements* but did nothing to create an efficient and reliable process for implementing those requirements. They did not invest into architecting the assembly line; they simply put engineers on it and told them to start coding. The engineers did the best they could, under the circumstances, and you already know how it ended.

I hope I convinced you that architecting against the functional spec for the final sellable product or service isn't nearly enough. It doesn't address the main purpose of the software architecture in the first place. It does quite the opposite – instead of reducing the cost of future changes, an architecture that is based purely on the functional spec (or the lack of thereof) frequently necessitates future changes.

What exactly shall we consider, beyond the functional spec, when creating a software architecture? What are the right questions to ask ourselves when creating a blueprint for a new system?

Here is my personal hit list I compiled over the years. Your list might be larger. Reflect on it and expand as needed.

- Programming languages, their features, readability, and interoperation
- Code reuse across platforms (server vs web vs mobile)
- Early error detection (compile-time vs runtime error detection, breadth of validation)
- Availability and cost of hiring the right talent; learning curve for new hires
- Readability and refactorability of code
- Approach to code composition, embracing the change
- Datastore and general approach to data modeling
- Application-specific data model, and the blast radius from changing it
- Performance and latency in all tiers and platforms
- Scalability and redundancy
- Spiky traffic patterns, autoscaling, capacity planning
- Error recovery
- Logging, telemetry, and other instrumentation
- Reducing complexity
- User interfaces and their maintainability
- External APIs
- User identity and security
- Hardware and human costs of the infrastructure and its maintenance
- Enabling multiple concurrent development workstreams
- Enabling testability
- Fast-tracking development by adopting third-party frameworks

By considering every item on this list early, we have a chance to make fundamentally correct choices for our future architecture. Ideally, you should have an answer to every item on that list before a single line of code is written.

The rest of the book will walk you through making the pivotal decisions and selection of the design patterns necessary to address the hit list. The recipes I provide will not always match 1:1 to the items on the list, simply because some solutions address multiple items, and some provide only partial answers. As a whole, however, you will have a collection of recipes which answers every concern from the hit list and will invariably make you a better software architect.

<tldr>

Add your own considerations to the hit list from this chapter. Then make sure that the entire hit list is addressed by your architecture.

https://anatoly.com/the-architects-hit-list

</tldr>

CHAPTER 2
PROGRAMMING LANGUAGES

'Meow' means 'woof' in cat.
– George Carlin

I don't want us to get in the fight over your favorite programming language. You have the right to have your favorite dog, your favorite niece, your favorite golf clubs, and your favorite pizza place. You also have the right to have your favorite programming language – as long as this is strictly personal. However, the moment you start talking business, there is no room for favorites. In business, you have to be 100% logical in your choices of tooling. And the first choice you must make for any new project is the choice of a programming language. It will affect everything. Because of that, please put your feelings aside, and let me walk you through the cold and heartless selection process.

The diversity of the languages is tremendous. Just for fun, here are a few examples of a *Hello World* program, written in some of the popular languages.

Unix Shell

```
<code>
#!/bin/bash
STR="Hello World!"
echo $STR
</code>
```

C

```
<code>
#include <stdio.h>
int main(void) {
  printf("hello, world\n");
}
</code>
```

C++

```
<code>
#include <iostream>
int main() {
  std::cout << "Hello, world!\n";
  return 0;
}
</code>
```

C#

```
<code>
using System;
class HelloWorld {
  static void Main(string[] args) {
    Console.WriteLine("Hello, world!");
  }
}
</code>
```

Java

```
<code>
class HelloWorld {
  public static void main(String[] args) {
    System.out.println("Hello World!");
  }
}
</code>
```

JavaScript

```
<code>
console.log("Hello World!");
</code>
```

Objective-C

```
<code>
main() {
  puts("Hello World!");
  return 0;
}
</code>
```

Python

```
<code>
 print("Hello World")
</code>
```

PHP

```
<code>
 <?php echo "Hello, World";
</code>
```

Ruby

```
<code>
 puts 'Hello World!'
</code>
```

Go

```
<code>
 package main
 import "fmt"
 func main() {
   fmt.Println("Hello, World")
 }
</code>
```

Even through these primitive examples, you can get a good sense of how readable and how verbose the code might be. But of course, the influence of the programming language goes much deeper. Here are the characteristics of languages I find of utter importance: *strong static typing*, *explicitly defined data structures*, *interfaces*, *isomorphism*, *third party libraries*, *ease of refactoring*, *functional vs object-oriented*, *ease and cost of hiring*, *learning curve for new hires*, *general readability*. Let's have a look at each one.

Strong static typing. Programming languages are generally divided by *strong vs weak typing*, and by *static vis dynamic type checking*. *Strong typing* essentially means that the language imposes strict restrictions on intermixing values of different data types.

Consider this example in JavaScript:

```
<code>
// balance is of type string
let balance = "10";
// interestRate is of type number
let interestRate = 0.05;
...
let newBalance = balance + balance * interestRate;
// prints 100.5 (as string value)
console.log( newBalance );
</code>
```

The resulting value of `100.5` for `newBalance` is unexpected. The same code, when rewritten in TypeScript, produces an error in the line calculating `newBalance`:

```
<code>
// balance is of type string
let balance = "10";

// interestRate is of type number
let interestRate = 0.05;
...
// the following line causes an error
let newBalance = balance + balance * interestRate;
console.log( newBalance );
</code>
```

TypeScript also gives you an ability to specify the intended types of each variable, like this:

```
<code>
// the following line causes an error
let balance : number = "10";

// interestRate is of type number
let interestRate : number = 0.05;
...
let newBalance : number = balance + balance * interestRate;
console.log( newBalance );
</code>
```

When the type of a variable is explicitly specified, then the error is caught early, pinpointing at the root cause. In our example, it's the attempt to assign a string value to a numeric variable.

Intermixing values of different data types is among the top causes of software bugs, and strong typing helps to catch them early, and to pinpoint the root cause.

The other important distinction between languages is *static vs dynamic type checking*. Languages with the static type checking detect errors at compile time, without running the code. Languages with dynamic type checking detect errors at runtime, when the execution reaches the statement which exhibits the problem. Consider this example in Python:

```
price : float = 10.00 # the price is a floating-point number
if blue_moon: # occurs rarely
  price = "abc" # the price is now a string
# the tax calculation line may result in runtime error:
# can't multiply sequence by non-int of type 'float'
tax : float = price * 0.08
print( tax )
```

Here, the price is a floating-point numeric value, but once in a blue moon (when blue_moon is True) it is set to a string value, making the tax calculation crash. Since the blue moon is rare, the crash is highly unlikely to be caught during testing. This is a ticking bomb in your code. It eventually will blow up, at a much later time in production. BTW, if you rewrite this code in JavaScript, the result will be even worse, because the code will not crash, but will produce a NaN (not-a-number) value, making the problem even harder to catch.

Consider the same code, now in TypeScript, which has static type checking.

```
let price : number = 10.00; // the price is of type number
if( blue_moon ) { // occurs rarely, not encountered in testing
  price = `abc`; // compile time error
}
let tax = price * 0.08;
console.log( tax );
```

Here, the error is detected at compile time. No testing necessary, no time wasted, no risk to the production system.

<important>

To produce reliable code, you need a language featuring both strong typing and static type checking. Apologies to all JavaScript and Python lovers.

</important>

Support for explicitly defined data structures. This refers to the language's ability to define a data structure and validate compliance of the objects you create against that declaration at compile time. This usually takes shape of *interfaces* or *classes*. Validations against declared object structure allow you to catch errors at compile time before you even run the code. This accelerates development and creates more stable software. Since testing of a large system never has 100% coverage, the more can be checked at compile time the better.

Consider this example in JavaScript:

```
<code>
  const printAddress = (
    user
  ) => {
    console.log( `Dear ${user.firstName} ${user.lastName}!` );
  };

  // Dear John Smith!
  printAddress( { firstName: `John`, lastName: `Smith` } );

  // Dear John undefined
  printAddress( { firstName: `John`, typo: `Smith` } );
</code>
```

Here, the member of the data structure representing a user is accidentally mistyped (entered `typo` instead of `lastName`) and the error is relatively hard to catch; it requires very attentive testing.

Now let's look at how this problem is fixed in TypeScript:

```
<code>
  const printAddress = (
    user : { firstName : string, lastName : string }
  ) => {
    console.log( `Dear ${user.firstName} ${user.lastName}!` );
  };

  // Dear John Smith!
  printAddress( { firstName: `John`, lastName: `Smith` } );

  // compile time error
  printAddress( { firstName: `John`, typo: `Smith` } );
</code>
```

Here, the structure of the `user` argument is explicitly declared, and the typo is caught at compile time.

Better, when using an Integrated Development Environment (IDE), it will automatically highlight the error in your source code as you type:

```
const printAddress = (
  user : { firstName : string, lastName : string }
) : void  => {
  console.log( `Dear ${ user.firstName } ${ user.lastName }!` );
};

// Dear John Smith!
printAddress(  user: { firstName : `John`, lastName : `Smith` } );

// compile time error
printAddress(  user: { firstName : `John`, typo : `Smith` } );
```

Modern IDEs take it further by performing static code analysis and suggesting valid data members as you type your code in. Here is an example in which the IDE (IntelliJ IDEA) "knows" that you already entered firstName, and still missing lastName.

```
const printAddress = (
  user : { firstName : string, lastName : string }
) : void  => {
  console.log( `Dear ${ user.firstName } ${ user.lastName }!` );
};

// Dear John Smith!
printAddress(  user: { firstName : `John`, lastName : `Smith` } );

// compile time error
printAddress(  user: { firstName : `John`, } );
              @ lastName (data-structure-01.ts)     string
              Press ⏎ to insert, → to replace                    ⋮
```

<important>

Explicitly defined data structures in statically typed languages increase both development velocity and reliability of software. Velocity can be further improved by using a modern IDE.

</important>

Support for interfaces. This refers to the language support for the *interface* feature, which is a way to create an *abstraction*, or *contract*, for a data structure or a class. Interfaces are important because they enable the so-called *Dependency Injection* design pattern and support a broader *Dependency Inversion Principle*. We will look at this closer when discussing Code Composition guidelines (Chapter 6). For now, it suffices to say that interfaces allow you to work with a software component by referring to its "contract", while knowing nothing about the component's internal implementation.

Here is an example:

```
<code>
interface Logger {
  log( value : string ) : void;
};
const foo = ( logger : Logger ) : void => {
  logger.log( `entered function foo` );
};
</code>
```

Here, the implementation of function foo() writes to the log having no knowledge of how the logger is implemented. We can now implement the logger in several different ways, with no changes in foo(). For instance:

```
<code>
const myLogger : Logger = {
  log( value : string ) : void {
    console.log( `*** ${ value }` );
  }
};
foo( myLogger );
</code>
```

Now you have the flexibility of supplying different loggers to foo(). For instance, one logger may automatically print the date and time of every logged event, and another may send all logging data to a server of your choice for storage and processing. The foo() function remains unchanged as long as the contract for the logger implementation (the Logger interface) stays the same.

What if your language does not support interfaces? An inferior solution is to use abstract classes to define contracts. This will work in languages which supports abstract classes and inheritance, but have no interfaces, like Python.

<important>

Support for interfaces is cornerstone to many principles of software architecture and code composition.

</important>

Isomorphism. This refers to the language's ability to run across multiple platforms that underpin your solution. In the most common scenario, that's the ability of the language to run on the client platform (browser and/or mobile devices) and on the server. I distinguish three levels of language's isomorphic qualities.

Native isomorphism means the language works on all target platforms natively. For instance, JavaScript works both in the browser and on the server as is. It also means that all the third-party libraries are available for that language across all platforms[1].

Transpiled isomorphism means the language is not supported across all platforms natively but can be *transpiled* (cross-compiled) into another language which is natively isomorphic. An example of such language is TypeScript; it transpiles into JavaScript, which can be executed by a browser on the client side, by Node.js on the server side, and can be used for mobile apps if they are developed with React Native or Apache Cordova. Transpiled isomorphism, just like native isomorphism, allows you to use the same third-party libraries across all platforms.

Generated isomorphism means the language is not supported across all platforms natively, but there exists a tool that generates platform-specific code in another language, independently for each platform. A good example is Kotlin, which can run natively on a server in a Java Virtual Machine or on Android devices, but also can generate a JavaScript equivalent to run in a browser. This is the weakest kind of isomorphism because it makes your code portable but it would not port third party libraries that you may need, unless they are written in the same language and are supplied with the source code. For instance, Kotlin can be compiled into JavaScript, but third-party libraries would have to be supplied with the source code in Kotlin to be portable. If you use JDK or any other library distributed as a binary, it will not be transpiled into JavaScript, for the lack of the source code. This makes generated isomorphism somewhat limited in real life applications.

Generally speaking, both Native and Transpiled levels of isomorphism are sufficient for most projects. The most popular native option is JavaScript, because

---

[1] With the obvious exception of platform-specific functionality.

it is the only language that natively runs in any browser, on the server in Node.js, and is usable for mobile development with Cordova and React Native. However, due to its other drawbacks, such as the lack of support for strong static typing and interfaces, I prefer TypeScript, which is compatible with everything JavaScript plus adds the missing strong static typing, interfaces, and a number of other awesome features.

<important>

Native and Transpiled Isomorphic languages are extremely useful in cross-platform development, by allowing you to share your code and third-party libraries across platforms.

</important>

Availability of third-party libraries. The widely used languages enjoy broad third-party support. For instance, there is probably an NPM module for everything under the sun, putting JavaScript and TypeScript amongst the most supported languages. More "esoteric" languages may force you into writing additional code to compensate for the lack of pre-existing solutions. The languages which currently enjoy the broadest third-party support are JavaScript/TypeScript, Java, and Python.

<important>

You don't have to write everything by yourself. Your choice of language will affect your ability to use third-party libraries.

</important>

Ease of refactoring. *Refactoring means restructuring of existing code without changing its external behavior.* Refactoring helps improve readability and reduce complexity and is the main instrument of migration to new or updated data models. Typical refactoring operations include *renaming data types, variables and members, moving members from one class to another, adding or removing parameters to functions, converting methods to top-level functions, converting static members to global variables or constants, converting inner classes to top-level classes, moving declarations and implementations between modules*, and numerous others.

Without solid refactoring tools, changes to the architecture often become cost prohibitive. Refactoring tools are usually stronger with compiled languages with strong static type checking, since they allow for reliable static code analysis. Java has excellent refactoring support, especially when using popular IDEs like Eclipse or IntelliJ IDEA. On the other side of the spectrum, I wasn't able to find adequate refactoring tools for Python or PHP.

<important>

Make sure your language creates a good foundation for future refactoring. A good IDE for your language with strong support for refactoring can make a huge difference.

</important>

Functional vs Object-Oriented. For a long time, *object-oriented* way of writing code was the holy grail of software engineering. But recently, more architects realize that, while some of the object-oriented principles are golden, some others cause more harm than good – and started rediscovering and leaning more and more towards *functional programming (FP)*[2]. Let's briefly look at the two paradigms[3].

Object-Oriented Programming (OOP) paradigm works with objects, which are usually stateful. OOP claims that bringing together the data and its associated behaviors in a single location (an object) makes it easier to understand the code. OOP promotes *encapsulation*, which is essentially an approach which treats any object (i.e., data plus behavior) as a "black box". And OOP introduces *inheritance*, which helps write less code when implementing objects with significant similarities, and *interfaces*, which are clearly defined contracts for the objects to comply with. Interfaces provide foundation for *Dependency Injection* pattern, which we already listed earlier as a must-have.

Functional Programming (FP) says that the data and behaviors are distinctively different things and should be kept separate for clarity. In contrast with OOP's approach to encapsulation, FP treats behaviors as "black box", while treating data as "white box". FP advocates stateless implementation of behaviors, which are expressed as "pure" functions – i.e., functions that cause no side effects. Pure functions are not supposed to change their parameters or their environment, and the only effect of running a pure function is the returned result. Clearly, you can't have

---

[2] FP is a fairly old concept that predates OOP, but its practical applications were limited due to the cryptic syntax of the early functional languages (think LISP).

[3] I will not attempt to fully explain OOP and FP here. We are merely going to look into those few traits that make a difference for reaching fundamental architectural decisions.

all the code written as pure functions, or otherwise that code will have no effect whatsoever, and you have to violate this paradigm at some point.

Which approach is better? There is no single definitive answer; it really depends on what we are modeling. Generally speaking, OOP works better when we are modeling real-life objects which behaviors are mostly defined on the data stored in those objects and require little interaction with the rest of the environment. For instance, a space probe flying through the void with no interaction with other objects in space can be cleanly modeled as an object with behaviors (methods) which manipulate its engines for maneuvering in space. But try modeling a pool ball that bounces off other balls and off the rails, and you will quickly find that behaviors no longer naturally apply to a single object, and OOP falls short of its promise.

The other downfall of OOP paradigm is ironically rooted in one of its most advertised features – *inheritance*. Modeling of an application domain as a hierarchy of classes is only successful in the long term when the domain is well understood and is stable. In the real world, however, the initially designed model is merely a crude approximation of the reality, and it is refined over time, as the business learns from the market and evolves. In the process, the initially apparent similarities of objects that went into the original inheritance model frequently disappear, replaced by a new, better understanding and a better model. Changing an inheritance-based model usually requires major refactoring effort and carry high costs and significant business risks. This problem in practice is compounded by frequent attempts to achieve polymorphic behavior and code reuse through inheritance instead of composition[4].

FP paradigm, on the other hand, is frequently misunderstood and is rarely enforced by programming languages. Most of the languages that support FP do not enforce "purity" of functions and require a lot of discipline to reap the true benefits promised by FP. The only purely functional programming language I know is Haskell – have you ever heard of it? If not, you are not alone; it is far from being mainstream.

Most of the programming languages nowadays strive to support both paradigms, but usually fall short on delivering both equally well. For instance, Java (originally

---

[4] In other words, there is a confusion between *is-a* (inheritance) vs *has-a* (composition) relationships between classes. The inheritance pattern is used instead of composition because most OOP languages do not have the syntactical sugar to make composition as convenient as inheritance.

an OOP language) was retrofitted with *lambda functions*[5] which promise the use of functions similar to that of JavaScript or TypeScript, but still, lambda functions are not true first-class citizens in Java; their use is somewhat limited and verbose. Java also received an upgrade in the form of Stream API, which provides a very "functional" way of handling sequences of objects. On the other hand, JavaScript (originally non-OOP language) now has the syntactical sugar to define classes, but despite the apparent similarities, the underlying prototypal inheritance behaves very differently from the classical OOP inheritance.

When choosing the language for your project, you must consider the desired paradigm, as well as your ability to enforce such paradigm through your architecture and frameworks. If you are not prescriptive about the coding style, then every member of your team will act out of their past experience, which is likely to create undesirable inconsistencies in code composition and style.

I personally find it helpful to use the best of both worlds. I believe that the use of interfaces, and interface inheritance typical to OOP languages, is fundamental to decoupling. I also find that class inheritance frequently does more harm than good in business applications. Traditional functional programming syntax in the likes of Lisp, Haskell or Clojure are unreadable to an untrained eye. Having said that, I love the concept of "pure" functions to create predictable and highly readable code.

<important>

Invest the time into understanding both OOP and FP. Take the best of both worlds. Pick languages that support the features you are looking for.

</important>

Ease and cost of hiring. At the time of this writing, Python engineers are the easiest to find and are less expensive than Java engineers. While these trends shift, consider your financial ability to staff your team before making a language decision[6].

---

[5] Not to be confused with AWS Lambda

[6] This piece of advice caused quite a bit of rebuke from my reviewers. A seasoned engineering manager noted that, over the past 10 years, he came to the conclusion that Python lowers the barrier of entry to software development, and as a side effect of that it lowers the level of software engineering prowess of an average Python programmer to be well below the industry average.

For large projects, consider job market while deciding on the programming language.

</important>

Learning curve. Not all your new hires will necessarily be experts in the language of your choice. You may hire people for their domain expertise as a primary requirement. How long will it take an "uninitiated" developer to become productive? For instance, Python has proven itself as one of the easiest languages to learn, while Forth and Prolog are extremely hard to wrap one's head around.

<important>

Make sure you can quickly train junior engineers to code in the language of your choice.

</important>

Readability. This is a fairly vague and subjective characteristic, which is referring to how easy it is to discern the business logic by looking at the code. It is hard to quantify, especially with the interference from variations of coding styles - but I think we can all agree that reading code in assembly language or Forth is harder than Java. Generally speaking, readability is directly related to (a) how closely the language is modeled after the human language (i.e., how closely the programming language follows the flow of an informal spec written in, say, English), and (b) how much semantic value is assigned to non-verbal constructs (punctuation, special characters, indentation, etc.) Historically, one of the most readable languages of all times was COBOL (if you look up a few code samples, then you will immediately see why – but it was way too verbose to the tastes of a contemporary developer).

<important>

Make sure the language of your choice is easily readable. Give a piece of code to a developer who "speaks" the language but unfamiliar with the purpose of the code and see if they can quickly grasp what that code does.

I listed some of the most popular languages for business application development in the table below, alongside with how they score against the various criteria we discussed earlier[7].

	Java	Kotlin	JavaScript	TypeScript	Python
Explicit data structures	Yes	Yes	No	Yes	No
Strong static typing	Yes	Yes	No	Yes	No[8]
Interfaces	Yes	Yes	No	Yes	No
Isomorphism	No (server and Android native) Generated for browser with GWT framework	Generated (server and Android native, browser generated)	Native (server and browser native, Android+iOS native with React Native, or hybrid with Cordova)	Transpiled (server and browser native, Android+iOS native with React Native or hybrid with Cordova)	No (server native)
OOP vs FP	OOP first	OOP first	FP first	FP first + interfaces	OOP first
Third party libraries	Many	Few	Many	Many	Many
Refactoring	Strong	Strong	Weak	Medium	Weak
Hiring	Expensive	Expensive, hard to find	Inexpensive, easy to find	Inexpensive, easy to find	Inexpensive, easy to find
Learning curve	Medium	Steep	Flat	Flat	Flat
Readability	Great	Medium	Medium	Medium	Poor

---

[7] If you disagree with my assessments, feel free to fill out this table on your own, and come to your own conclusions. What's important in the language selection is to be driven by pure logic and business interests, and not by personal attachments formed by the past experiences.

[8] Starting from Python 3.6 there is a way to include data type names into variable declarations, but the language still has a long way to go to match the validation level of TypeScript or Java.

Edit the table if you disagree with my assessments. Expand it with the languages you consider for your project. Then decide which languages you should be using going forward.

To help you with decision making for your next project, consider several archetypal use cases from the table below. All use cases listed assume the following:

- a need to have server-side implementation;
- a need to have web-based user interface;
- a need to build mobile apps for iOS and Android platforms.

Use Case	Language Choices
Strictly optimize for cost and time.	• TypeScript server-side. • TypeScript with React/Redux shared code between web client and Cordova hybrid mobile apps for iOS and Android.
Maximize reliability of server-side code, then optimize for cost & time.	• Java server-side; consider Kotlin or Scala as more expensive options. • Protobufs IDL • TypeScript with React/Redux shared code between web client and Cordova hybrid mobile apps for iOS and Android.
Provide smooth native user experience in mobile apps, then optimize for cost & time.	• TypeScript server-side. • TypeScript with React/Redux for web client. • TypeScript with React Native or Flutter/Dart shared code between native mobile apps for iOS and Android.
Maximize reliability of server-side code, provide smooth native user experience in mobile apps, then optimize for cost & time.	• Java server-side; consider Kotlin or Scala as more expensive options. • Protobufs IDL • TypeScript with React/Redux for web client. • TypeScript with React Native or Flutter/Dart shared code between native mobile apps for iOS and Android.

The choice of programming language isn't obvious and shall not be taken lightly. Consider strong static typing, support of interfaces, isomorphism, OOP vs FP capabilities, readability, third-party support, and the cost of hiring.

https://anatoly.com/programming-languages

CHAPTER 3
DATASTORE

Not only do I not know what's going on, I wouldn't know what to do about it if I did.
   – George Carlin

One day, I gave my team a puzzle to solve.

"Let's have some fun," I said. "Imagine that you mentally divide your system into three large components: *User Interface*, *Business Logic*, and *Datastore*. Now think of which component depend on which."

Tom, always pedantic with definitions, asked:

"Could you please define *dependency?*"

That made me think for a moment. Then I said:

"Let's say that component A *depends on* component B if the changes made to component B may trigger a need to change component A. Such dependencies are frequently expressed in the code as *import* statements, i.e., component A *depends on* component B if it *imports* one or several interfaces or classes or functions from component B."

"That's easy," Tom said. "The User Interface depends on the Business Logic, and the Business Logic depends on the Datastore." He picked a marker and drew a diagram on the whiteboard:

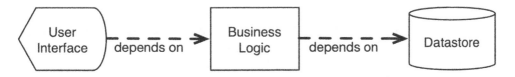

I agreed with the User Interface dependency but wasn't buying the rest.

"Why do you think the Business Logic must depend on the Datastore?" I asked.

"Simple," Tom said happily. "The Datastore must be the most stable component in the system, thus the Business Logic must depend on it."

"Why must the Datastore be the most stable component?" I kept digging.

The response was instantaneous, from the entire team, as if they rehearsed for hours in anticipation of this very moment:

"Because the Datastore is the hardest to change. When you change your database structure, you break all the code that accesses the data, potentially the entire system," they chanted. "The Datastore must be protected from change at all costs, and therefore the Business Logic must depend on it, and work with whatever data model is offered by the Datastore."

OMG. They fell straight into the trap.

"Well," I said, "which component is the most important part of your system?"

"Business Logic, I suppose…" Tom was the first to see the trap door closing.

"Correct," I said. "The entire reason the system exists is its Business Logic. The goal of building the system is not the specifics of the user interface, and not the Datastore structure either. The system does something that generates revenue or something else of importance, and that *something* is coded in your Business Logic. The Business Logic is king, and everything else is there to serve it. Because of that, both User Interface and Datastore must depend on the Business Logic, and not the other way around."

I corrected the dependency diagram:

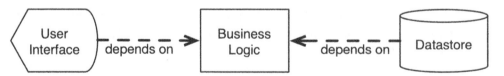

"But then… how are we going to deal with the fact that the Datastore is hard to change, and that changing it breaks everything?" Tom was not letting me off the hook either.

"Well, we have to *architect* the Datastore the right way."

Let's take a closer look at what options we have. The first thing that comes to mind is to use a noSQL database, instead of a traditional RDBMS. In general, schema-less databases indeed help make changes to the Datastore less daunting, and many architects opt for that solution. This is more of a band-aid than a real solution, and we are going to pass on noSQL as a sole remedy, in favor of a proper architecture of the Datastore.

First, let's deal with the nature of dependencies. As mentioned earlier, they are usually expressed as import statements in your code. Consider this example.

Datastore code:

```
// module datastore.ts

export interface UserProfile {
  userId : string;
  firstName : string;
  lastName : string;
  age : number;
};

export const readUserProfile = ( userId : string ) : UserProfile => {
  … // read user from the database
};
```

Business Logic code:

```
// module business-logic.ts

import { readUserProfile, UserProfile } from './datastore';

const printUser = ( userId : string ) : void => {
  let user : UserProfile = readUserProfile( userId );
  console.log( `user: ${ user.userId } ${ user.firstName }` );
};
```

The above example represents the incorrect dependency: the business logic imports a data structure and a method defined by the Datastore. To fix this, we will use the technique called *Dependency Inversion*[9]. We will be discussing this technique more than once in this book. For now, let's learn by example. Let's consider this alternative implementation.

---

[9] If you are unfamiliar with the concept of Dependency Inversion, refer to Appendix I before you continue.

Business Logic code, module `business-logic-defs`:

```
<code>
// module business-logic-defs.ts

export interface UserProfile {
  userId : string;
  firstName : string;
  lastName : string;
  age : number;
};

export interface UserDataAccess {
  readUserProfile( userId : string ) : UserProfile;
};
</code>
```

Business Logic code, module `business-logic-impl`:

```
<code>
// module business-logic-impl.ts

import { UserDataAccess, UserProfile } from './business-logic-defs';

const printUser = ( da : UserDataAccess, userId : string ) : void => {
  let user : UserProfile = da.readUserProfile( userId );
  console.log( `user: ${ user.userId } ${ user.firstName }` );
};
</code>
```

Datastore code:

```
<code>
// module datastore.ts

import { UserDataAccess, UserProfile } from './business-logic-defs';

export class UserDataAccessImpl implements UserDataAccess {
  readUserProfile( userId: string ) : UserProfile {
    … // read user from the database
  }
};
</code>
```

What has just happened? We inverted the dependency. Now, the Datastore imports the definitions from Business Logic. From now on, Business Logic dictates what it wants from the Datastore, and the Datastore must obey. And now, whenever Business Logic changes or expands, the Datastore must adjust accordingly – and not the other way around.

<important>
Both User Interface and Datastore must depend on the Business Logic.
</important>

The above line of reasoning leaves out the potential complexity of changing the Datastore. We will tackle that next. For that, we will look into one of the most pivotal architectural decisions – the organization of your data persistence. There are several popular approaches which we will consider: *CRUD*, *CQRS*, and *Event Store*.

CRUD stands for *Create, Read, Update, Delete*. This is a mainstream approach, intended to continuously maintain the current state of the application in the Datastore. CRUD comes from the days of scarce computing resources, limited disk space, and slow databases. Let's use a simplistic shopping cart implementation as an example. It is frequently modeled in CRUD paradigm as a set of records, each record representing an item placed in the shopping cart. Adding an item to the cart is implemented by creating a new record. Removing an item from the cart is implemented by deleting a record. Updating quantity is implemented as updating a record for the respective cart item. The beauty of CRUD is that it provides you with the latest state of the application with minimal effort. For instance, to display the contents of the shopping cart from our example, you simply read all the records for the cart, and it will give you the latest state, ready to be displayed to an end user.

CRUD paradigm is usually mapped into a programming language as a set of Create, Read, Update, and Delete operations, each acting on a predefined data structure that represents a database record. And that's where an inherent design flaw is hiding. Let's go back to our shopping cart example. Assuming a typical relational database implementation, you end up having two tables, Cart and CartItem, as depicted here:

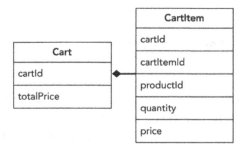

What you may quickly notice is that we must update the Cart record every time we manipulate CartItem, to maintain the correct value of totalPrice. This is inefficient. A much better solution is to exclude totalPrice from the Cart altogether and recompute it every time when the Cart is retrieved, by iterating over CartItem records. Another observation is that the price for CartItem could be also calculated automatically, and cartItemId could be auto generated. Finally, we might want to limit the update of a cart item to only updating the quantity field. But such changes break the traditional CRUD paradigm which performs all four operations (Create, Read, Update, and Delete) using the same data structure.

CQRS stands for *Command Query Responsibility Segregation*, and it is specifically designed to solve this problem. In contrast with CRUD, CQRS has two data models instead of one. The first model, known as *Query Model*, is responsible for retrieval of data (Read action from CRUD). The second model, known as *Command Model*, manipulates the data by processing *commands*. Commands could be the already familiar Create, Update, and Delete operations from CRUD, but CQRS allows you to define as many commands as you like, of any kind.

Here is how the data model for our shopping cart example could be constructed using CQRS:

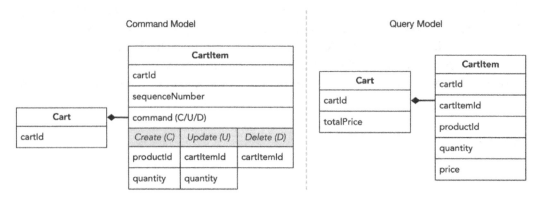

Notice how the `totalPrice` and the `price` are now available from the Query Model only; they are now intended to be automatically calculated. Also, notice how different commands in the Command Model accept only the data relevant to each individual command; this certainly adds clarity to the interface.

The two models describe the *interfaces* you use to represent your data and the operations on it; they do not dictate how the data is actually stored in the database. One of the practical implementations of CQRS stores all the *commands* which come through the Command Model directly in the database; such implementation is called **Event Store**, *Command Store*, or sometimes *Immutable Store*. The current state of the application is not recorded, only *events* (aka *commands*) are recorded. In our example with the shopping cart, we can record all the operations performed by the user on the cart. Every time a user adds an item to the cart, removes an item, or changes quantity, the respective event is recorded. Query Model continues to represent the current state of the application, but now, instead of reading the state directly from the database, it reconstructs the state by "replaying" the recorded sequence of events.

Since events are only added to the database but are never physically updated or deleted, the database is used in append-only mode – hence the name *Immutable Store*. Append-only databases usually scale better, have less locking and transaction isolation challenges, and open up a wide variety of storage options beyond traditional relational engines.

For certain types of businesses, immutability comes naturally. For instance, banking data with credits and debits posted to an account is essentially a history of credit/debit events. Almost all accounting data models are built on the *immutability principle: once something is recorded into the datastore, it never changes*. If a credit or debit was recorded in error, you must record an adjustment as a separate event. This makes accounting software incredibly reliable, and the entire history of transactions is always available for inspection.

The Event Store pattern is depicted in this diagram:

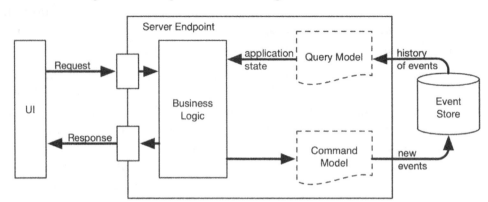

Note that when Query Model computes the application state from the history of events, it doesn't have to consider the entire history of all events since the dawn of time. That would be incredibly impractical. It only needs to consider the events which affect the requested portion of the application state. For instance, when Business Logic requests the content of a shopping cart, the Query Model only needs the events pertaining to one specific shopping cart, for one particular user, since the last order was placed by that user. This significantly reduces the amount of data for the Query Model to receive and process. At the same time, it imposes a requirement on the Event Store to support the necessary event queries efficiently.

What's interesting about this approach is that Query Model may use the same stored events to construct a variety of application states, following different models. Think of it as an ability to create different "views" into the application's state. Why is it important? First, having different ways of looking at the data is useful for different types of work. For instance, the data model servicing users online may differ from the model used for business intelligence and from the model used for accounting. Second, it helps making your datastore more pliable. Remember the dependency diagram from the earlier in this chapter? Let me refresh your memory:

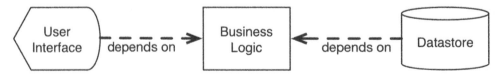

At the time, we concluded that the Datastore must be able to accommodate a change in Business Logic with ease but haven't discussed how. Event Store is our silver bullet. It allows us to modify the model without restructuring the stored data. We can use the same stored events to construct whatever model we want. This gives us far more flexibility in responding to changes in Business Logic than a traditional persistent application state.

But we must also consider performance. By making the Query Model rebuild the application state every time, we create much higher load on the database. Also, there are use cases when new events come in often and in large numbers. This may require the Event Store to process too many events at once, resulting in poor online performance. For example, imagine if your bank must look into every transaction since you opened the account 10 years ago, just to display the account balance?

The solution to this is to maintain an *application state snapshot*. Consider the following diagram:

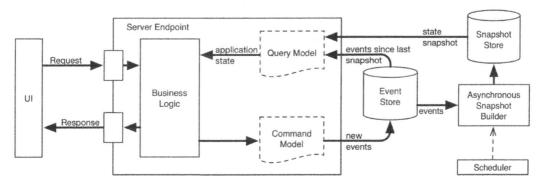

Here, we introduce a new component – the *Asynchronous Snapshot Builder* – which is executed periodically. Its purpose is to create the good old persistent state and to save it in the Snapshot Store. Essentially, the Asynchronous Snapshot Builder executes the same code as the Query Model does, to compute the latest application state. The Snapshot Store persists the state in a way which is convenient for the Query Model to retrieve. The Query Model then reads the latest snapshot, updates it further with events which arrived after the snapshot was built, and then serves up the final current state to the Business Logic.

This addresses the problem of the Query Model processing too many events. Now, it only has to process the events which arrived after the snapshot was created. Note that there is no strict requirement for the snapshot to contain the data. For instance, in our example with the bank account, we may decide to save only the account balance in the snapshot. However, if you go through the trouble of creating a full application state and storing it in a relational database, then your architecture becomes immediately compatible with myriad of third-party tools for reporting, analytics, ETL (extract-transform-load) tools, etc.

Keep in mind that your Snapshot Store can be rebuilt at any time, if your data model changes. You may also decide to maintain multiple Snapshot Stores with different data models, to be used for different purposes, or for backward compatibility with the components which you want to protect from changes.

<tldr>

Datastore implementation must depend on the Business Logic, and not the other way around. Ditch CRUD in favor of CQRS. Consider Event Store pattern for its flexibility.

https://anatoly.com/datastore

</tldr>

CHAPTER 4
DATA MODEL

> *I think people should be allowed to do anything they want. We*
> *haven't tried that for a while. Maybe this time it'll work*
> *– George Carlin*

Now that you selected a general approach to persisting your data, the next step is to adopt an approach and a process for *data modeling*. When I say *data modeling*, I am referring to designing a representation of your application's state for coding, or a *Data Model*. In traditional architectures, the data model is a collection of classes or functions that encapsulate retrieval and manipulation of data. The process of modeling is, respectively, the thought process you use to determine which classes and functions your data model should have.

For many architects, the process of data modeling is driven by intuition. However, there are well-formulated methodologies for approaching it more formally. For business applications, I recommend *Domain-Driven Design (DDD)*.

DDD is an approach to software architecture based on modeling of a real business through software abstractions. In this book, I am restricting DDD specifically to the purpose of data modeling[10].

Domain is a sphere of knowledge, influence, or activity in which your system operates. For example, GPS navigation apps operate in the *navigation domain*, and personal finance apps operate in the *finance domain*. Each domain has its own specialized *terminology*, and there are usually *subject matter experts* who understand the domain and its terminology well. You will need those subject matter experts to apply DDD (unless you are the subject matter expert yourself).

DDD approach to building a data model is to interview the subject matter experts and understand their terminology. To convey the terminology to engineers, subject matter experts are asked to create a document called *domain dictionary* (aka *glossary*). Then, the application requirements are defined in the language which

---

[10] I am not in favor of applying DDD beyond data modeling, although DDD claims to have much broader applicability. I am also dismissing some of the DDD concepts (for instance, repositories) which are generally incompatible with other methodologies advocated in this book (such as CQRS).

you and the experts mutually agree upon, based on the previously defined domain dictionary. Such language is called *ubiquitous language*, and it will be used collectively by you, your team, and the subject matter experts to communicate while building the architecture, implementing and operating the system.

Once the ubiquitous language is established, the next step is to create a functional specification for your future system. The specification document must use the ubiquitous language to be universally understood by all parties. The document naturally contains *verbs* and *nouns*. Don't take this concept literally. Verbs refer to anything that identifies with an action or a process. Nouns refer to anything that identifies with an object or a subject.

Nouns describe the elements of data which the application operates on. DDD classifies data as referenceable objects, or *entities*, and non-referenceable objects, or *values*. Here are some examples of entities: *user, order, shipment, support ticket, stock keeping unit (SKU)*. They are referenceable because they carry an identity which allows us to reference them: `userId` for a user, `orderNumber` for an order, `trackingNumber` for a shipment, etc. The examples of values are *phone number, email address, street address, first name, age*. Values do not exist on their own, and cannot be referenced; they can be only included into entities. Values could be simple (such as first name or age) or could be composite (i.e., containing multiple attributes, for instance street address containing street, city, zip code, and country). In contrast with entities, values have no distinct identity, they serve as attributes of an entity. For example, entity `User` may be composed of these values: `userId`, `firstName`, `lastName`, `emailAddress`, `phoneNumber`, and `shippingAddress`.

Entities can be grouped into *aggregates*. For instance, *order* is an entity, but it can also be an *aggregate*, which includes two entities: *order* and *order item*. Aggregates simplify the model by accessing the entire aggregate (i.e., all entities included in the aggregate) in a single operation by using the identity of its *root entity*. In our example, we can access the entire order with all its items by specifying an order number, i.e., the identity of an order, which is the root entity of the order aggregate.

This diagram illustrates those concepts:

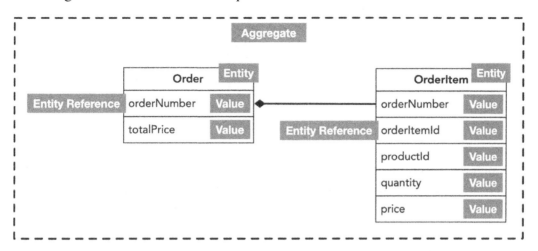

In the code, entities and aggregates are usually represented as interfaces or classes. For instance:

```
<code>
interface Order {
  orderNumber : number;
  totalPrice : number;
}

interface OrderItem {
  orderNumber : number;
  orderItemId : number;
  productId : string;
  quantity : number;
  price : number;
}

interface OrderAggregate {
  order : Order;
  orderItems : OrderItem[];
}
</code>
```

Verbs from the specification document describe *services*. From the coding perspective, services are interfaces containing methods, each method is a *verb*. Each service represents a meaningful piece of business logic described in the spec.

For instance:

```
<code>
interface BankingServices {
  openAccount(…);
  deposit(…);
  withdraw(…);
  transfer(…);
};
</code>
```

More often than not, your domain can be divided into several more or less independent sub-domains, aka *bounded contexts*. For instance, e-commerce domain can be divided into these bounded contexts: marketing, search, shopping, finance, fulfillment. For each of the bounded contexts, you can develop its own ubiquitous language and a respective data model, thus reducing the complexity of dealing with the entire domain into smaller sub-domains. On the highest domain level, the ubiquitous language will only describe integration matters.

<important>

The main idea behind DDD is to create a model in the software that closely follows the specification written in the ubiquitous language. The objects and services shall be clearly named after the business concepts, which makes the code easy to understand. As you discover new business requirements, your ubiquitous language grows, and the software model evolves alongside with it.

</important>

Let's consider an example – a simplistic cash-based single-currency banking system that manages accounts, and allows for deposits, withdrawals, and transfers between accounts, as well as balance inquiries. While interviewing an expert, we came up with the following ubiquitous language:

```
Account = list of ledger entries
Account Number = a unique identifier of an account
Credit = an operation of adding funds to an account
Debit = an operation of deducting funds from an account
Ledger Entry = a record of a debit or credit in an account
Ledger = a historical list of Ledger Entries for an account
Deposit = an operation of customer adding cash to their account
Withdrawal = an operation of customer removing cash from their account
Transfer = an operation of moving funds from one account to another
Amount = a monetary amount in USD currency, with decimal precision of 2
```

The specification for this system may look like this:

```
Create Account with Amount =
   new Account -> accountNumber
   Credit of Amount to Account

Deposit of Amount to Account =
   Credit of Amount to Account

Withdrawal of Amount from Account =
   Debit of Amount from Account

Transfer of Amount from Account1 to Account2 =
   Debit of Amount from Account1,
   Credit of Amount to Account2

Balance of Account =
   ( sum of all Credits to Account ) - ( sum of all Debits from Account )
```

Let's build a data model for the above specification. We will be using CQRS, but for simplicity will not be using event store (not yet). Instead, we will use a traditional relational database storing the latest application state.

First, the diagram depicting values, entities, and aggregates:

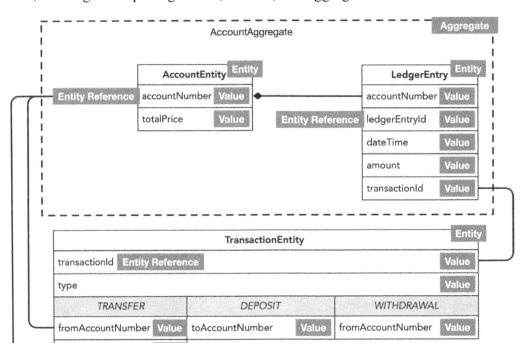

Here, we have the following entities: AccountEntity, LedgerEntry, and TransactionEntity. Each account may contain multiple ledger entries, representing the changes made to an account (debits and credits). For simplicity of data retrieval, we are combining AccountEntity and LedgerEntry into one AccountAggregate, so that the account information and all its ledger entries are retrieved in a single operation[11]. Transactions represent the operations performed by the end users. Transactions may affect one or several accounts, depending on the transaction type. In this example, we support three types of transactions: TRANSFER, DEPOSIT, and WITHDRAWAL. Transfer transactions move funds from one account to another; deposit transactions deposit cash into an account, and withdrawal transactions take cash out of an account.

---

[11] Don't build it this way in real life, unless you expect very low number of transactions during the lifetime of an account.

Next, let's translate this model into the code. At this point, we are not going to actually implement the data model but will only create contracts.

```
<code>
interface LedgerEntry {
  accountNumber : number;
  dateTime : Date;
  amount : number; // positive for credit, negative for debit
  transactionId : number; // refers to a transaction which produced the entry
};

interface AccountEntity {
  accountNumber : number;
  creationDateTime : Date;
  balance : number;
};

interface AccountAggregate {
  account : AccountEntity;
  ledgerEntries : LedgerEntry[];
};

enum TransactionType {
  DEPOSIT, WITHDRAWAL, TRANSFER
};

interface TransactionArgs {
};

interface DepositTransactionArgs extends TransactionArgs {
  toAccountNumber : number;
};

interface WithdrawalTransactionArgs extends TransactionArgs {
  fromAccountNumber : number;
};

interface TransferTransactionArgs extends TransactionArgs {
  fromAccountNumber : number;
  toAccountNumber : number;
};

interface TransactionEntity<T extends TransactionArgs> {
  transactionId : number;
  type : TransactionType;
  transactionArgs : T;
};

interface DepositTransactionEntity extends
TransactionEntity<DepositTransactionArgs> {
  type : TransactionType.DEPOSIT;
};
```

```
interface WithdrawalTransactionEntity extends
TransactionEntity<WithdrawalTransactionArgs> {
  type : TransactionType.WITHDRAWAL;
};
interface TransferTransactionEntity extends
TransactionEntity<TransferTransactionArgs> {
  type : TransactionType.TRANSFER;
};
interface CommandModel {
  createAccount() : { accountNumber : number };
  recordTransaction<T extends TransactionArgs >(
    transactionType : TransactionType,
    transactionArgs : T
  ) : { transactionId : number };
  recordLedgerEntry(
    accountId : number,
    amount : number,
    transactionId : number
  ) : void;
};
interface QueryModel {
  getAccount ( accountNumber : number ) : AccountAggregate;
  getTransaction( transactionId : string ) : TransactionEntity<any>;
};
</code>
```

It's easiest to untangle this code from the bottom up. Following CQRS guidelines, we ended up having two data models, CommandModel for modifying data, and QueryModel for retrieving data. CommandModel supports three operations: createAccount(), recordTransaction(), and recordLedgerEntry(). QueryModel supports getAccount() and getTransaction(). To support three types of transactions, we created interfaces for each type, all derived from the shared base interface TransactionEntity. We support three types of transactions: DepositTransaction, WithdrawalTransaction, and TransferTransaction. Notice the use of *generics* in TransactionEntity<T extends TransactionArgs>. If this syntax is unfamiliar or unclear, look up generics and how they work[12].

Everything we coded so far was based on the *nouns* from the specification representing the data. Now, let's move to the *verbs*. Our business logic is expressed

---

[12] Generics are fairly common in modern programming languages, such as TypeScript, Java, C#, and C++ (the latter has templates, which provide similar functionality). Generics are syntactical sugar intended to facilitate strong static typing, but you can do without them if your language of choice doesn't support them. For TypeScript, you can read about generics here: https://www.typescriptlang.org/docs/handbook/generics.html

in the form of four services: openAccount, deposit, withdraw, and transfer (all verbs). Let's start by defining the contract for our services:

```
interface Domain {
  commandModel : CommandModel;
  queryModel : QueryModel;
};

interface BankingServices {

  openAccount(
    domain : Domain
  ) : { newAccount : AccountAggregate };

  deposit(
    domain : Domain,
    toAccountNumber : number,
    amount : number
  ) : { toAccount : AccountAggregate };

  withdraw(
    domain : Domain,
    fromAccountNumber : number,
    amount : number
  ) : { fromAccount: AccountAggregate };

  transfer(
    domain : Domain,
    fromAccountNumber : number,
    toAccountNumber : number,
    amount : number
  ) : { fromAccount : AccountAggregate, toAccount : AccountAggregate }
};
```

Here, we defined the BankingServices interface, which requires four verbs to be implemented. Since BankingServices is a part of the application (business logic), it needs to access the data models and potentially other services from the domain layer. To avoid intermingling between the layers[13], we packaged the entire domain functionality into a single Domain interface, which is passed to every service call within BankingSerices as an argument.

---

[13] We will discuss this in finer detail in the next chapter.

Now that we defined the contract for banking services, we can proceed with the implementation:

```
<code>
const myBankingServices : BankingServices = {

  openAccount(
    domain : Domain
  ) : { newAccount : AccountAggregate } {
    let { accountNumber } = domain.commandModel.createAccount();
    return {
      newAccount : domain.queryModel.getAccount( accountNumber )
    };
  },

  deposit(
    domain : Domain,
    toAccountNumber: number,
    amount : number
  ) : { toAccount : AccountAggregate } {
    let { transactionId } =
      domain.commandModel.recordTransaction<DepositTransactionArgs>(
        TransactionType.DEPOSIT,
        { toAccountNumber : toAccountNumber }
      );
    domain.commandModel.recordLedgerEntry(
      toAccountNumber,
      amount,
      transactionId
    );
    return {
      toAccount : domain.queryModel.getAccount( toAccountNumber )
    };
  },

  withdraw(
    domain : Domain,
    fromAccountNumber: number,
    amount : number
  ) : { fromAccount : AccountAggregate } {
    let { transactionId } =
      domain.commandModel.recordTransaction<WithdrawalTransactionArgs>(
        TransactionType.WITHDRAWAL,
        { fromAccountNumber : fromAccountNumber }
      );
    domain.commandModel.recordLedgerEntry(
      fromAccountNumber,
      -amount,
      transactionId
    );
    return {
      fromAccount : domain.queryModel.getAccount( fromAccountNumber )
```

```
      };
    },
    transfer(
      domain : Domain,
      fromAccountNumber : number,
      toAccountNumber : number,
      amount : number
    ) : { fromAccount : AccountAggregate, toAccount : AccountAggregate } {
      let { transactionId } =
        domain.commandModel.recordTransaction<TransferTransactionArgs>(
          TransactionType.TRANSFER,
          {
            fromAccountNumber : fromAccountNumber,
            toAccountNumber : toAccountNumber
          },
        );
      domain.commandModel.recordLedgerEntry(
        fromAccountNumber,
        (-amount),
        transactionId
      );
      domain.commandModel.recordLedgerEntry(
        toAccountNumber,
        amount,
        transactionId
      );
      return {
        fromAccount : domain.queryModel.getAccount( fromAccountNumber ),
        toAccount : domain.queryModel.getAccount( toAccountNumber )
      };
    }
  };
```
</code>

Here, our implementation contains pure business logic, and nothing else. We are making use of the data models to access and manipulate the data, and each business function is concise enough to understand what it does at the first glance.

You may need to have your services interact with the outside world, for instance, to send mail, charge credit cards, ship purchased goods, etc. Those services should become a part of your domain and shall be represented by additional members of the Domain interface.

A good sanity check for a well-built model is to verify that your business logic operates purely within the terms defined by your ubiquitous language, and only manipulates the application's state and the outside world through the functionality exposed by the data model and by the consumed services. If any of your objects or services have no counterpart in the ubiquitous language, then you are likely mixing business concerns with technical ones, or your ubiquitous language is incomplete. Either way, this is a red flag. At this level, your code should be a direct mapping of the specification and must operate purely in business terms. This maximizes readability and maintainability of the code.

Finally, you may ask how the above approach changes if we incorporate an event store into our architecture. That changes everything, right? Wrong. If all is done right, there should be no changes to the contract of the data model at all, and the business logic should remain intact. The internal implementation of the data models will have to change, of course, but not the contracts. The contracts between the data models and the business logic remain unchanged. QueryModel retains its interface, although internally it retrieves the data from the latest persistent state snapshot and combines it with the more recent events. CommandModel is used to create the persistent state snapshot[14]. Finally, the business logic could be called not only by user actions, but also by the models to re-create the current application state by "replaying" the events.

<tldr>

Domain-Driven Design helps you create a data model that closely follows the business concepts, and therefore is easy to evolve alongside with the business requirements. Use CQRS to keep your interfaces clean.

https://anatoly.com/data-model

</tldr>

---

[14] The term "command model" may seem ambiguous, because now we have two command models: one that records the incoming events, and one that builds the persistent state snapshot. The command model from our example is the latter.

CHAPTER 5
LAYERING

One can never know for sure what a deserted area looks like.
– George Carlin

When software is developed without a layering strategy, developers are exposed to a complex and hard-to-grasp mixture of technologies. To reduce complexity, the software stack is usually broken down into several loosely coupled *layers*. Consider this diagram:

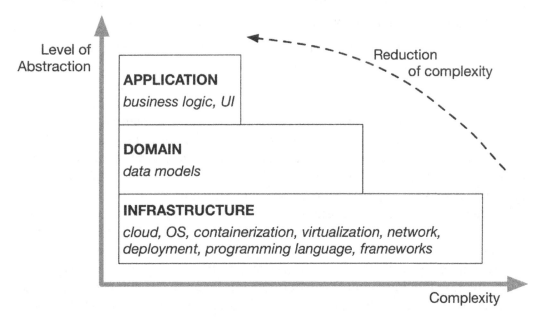

Here, we are limiting each software layer's respective responsibilities, which enables us to build an abstraction model for each layer. For the *infrastructure layer*, the abstraction model is usually provided to us in a form of a programming language, and myriad of libraries that provide access to cloud configuration, operating system, network, database, frameworks, third party libraries, etc. This layer exposes its functionality to the *domain layer* immediately above, which implements the data models, and exposes them to the *application layer*. The application layer focuses on the business logic and user interfaces. The domain can expose its functionality to the application in two popular ways: either as a set of interfaces or in a form of a *Domain-Specific Language* (DSL). When interfaces are used, then application is usually developed using the same general-purpose programming language (GPL) as the other layers. The DSL approach makes you create your own language, specific to your application domain, and then the entire application is built using that language. Notably, DSL does not have to be *imperative*[15], it can be purely *declarative*[16].

We are dealing with DLSs at all times, without necessarily realizing it. CSS is a declarative DSL for styling web content. HTML is a DSL for expressing a layout of a web page. XML is a DSL for organizing data. SQL is a DSL for manipulating data in a relational database. RegEx is a DSL for character pattern matching. Latex is a DSL for processing text. BPEL is a DSL for describing business processes. ACTULUS is a DSL for computing market values and cash flows.

A DSL need not take a shape and form of a text. It can be expressed as a table/spreadsheet, or as a user interface, or as a physical device. For instance, the front panel of a modern microwave oven "speaks" the language frequently used in the kitchen – such as cook, defrost, reheat, and may accept the weight in lbs. Internally, it converts this input into hardware-specific parameters such as power level and time. So instead of forcing the chef to compute the power and time parameters for thawing a steak, it accepts input in the ubiquitous language understood by any chef. This type of a DSL is the holy grail of domain-driven design: it allows the application to be written in the ubiquitous language itself, i.e. using the language of the business domain itself. Think of it as erasing the difference between the specification and the implementation. For instance, a cooking application can be written completely in the language of cooking recipes. A well implemented DSL allows subject matter experts create applications all by themselves, without involving engineers. Needless to say, the engineers are needed to create the DSL first. More often than not, however, DSLs are intended to be used by engineers – but save tons of time in the process.

---

[15] Imperative languages allow you to define a sequence of steps to be taken (an algorithm) for achieving the end result. A good example of an imperative languages are Java.
[16] Declarative languages allow you to specify the end result without having to specify an algorithm. A good example of a declarative language is SQL.

DSL is the ultimate solution to enforce a clean segregation of layers in your application. Naturally, when the application layer is coded in a DSL, and the domain layer is coded in a GPL, then the two will remain separated forever because of the differences in syntax and tooling.

In the interest of time and simplicity, architects frequently choose replacing a DSL with a set of objects and functions, which can be called from a "normal" general-purpose language. This saves time on development of a DSL and makes it easier to expand the domain services available to the application layer by simply adding more objects and functions. The DSL's replacement then is a library of those objects and functions. There is nothing terribly wrong with this idea, but it creates no natural barrier for developers to inadvertently cross layer boundaries. Over time, we start finding application code in the domain layer, and domain code in application layer – and once we do, it is already too late, and require significant refactoring effort to fix. Unfortunately, such refactoring will yield no immediate ROI for the business and could be challenging to budget. So – we need to find a way to keep all layers isolated, even if there is no DSL, and prevent intermingling of their respective functionality. This could be done either through a process, or through technology.

The process approach usually involves publishing strict rules and enforcing them through code reviews. In my experience, this approach carries cost-prohibitive overhead, unless there is a single developer on the project – you. The technology approach is in creating a restrictive framework, which confines developers to only specific set of interfaces they can interact with. Consider the earlier example of the hypothetical banking system, in which domain services are made available to the application layer through the Domain interface:

```
interface Domain {
  commandModel : CommandModel;
  queryModel : QueryModel;
};
```

The application can access the domain level functionality through the Domain interface only, which is passed as a parameter to any invocation of the application-level code, like this:

```
<code>
interface BankingServices {

  openAccount(
    domain : Domain
  ) : { newAccount : AccountAggregate };

  deposit(
    domain : Domain
    toAccountNumber : number,
    amount : number
  ) : { toAccount : AccountAggregate };

  withdraw(
    domain : Domain
    fromAccountNumber : number,
    amount : number
  ) : { fromAccount: AccountAggregate };

  transfer(
    domain : Domain
    fromAccountNumber : number,
    toAccountNumber : number,
    amount : number
  ) : { fromAccount : AccountAggregate, toAccount : AccountAggregate }

};
</code>
```

Here, every single one of BankingServices only gets to access the Domain. The implementers of BankingServices are now provided with all the tools they need through the domain argument, and we can prohibit them from using any services beyond those available through the Domain interface. If a need to create a new dependency arises, developers should ask the architect (you) to add new dependencies to the Domain interface. This process will keep you in control of runaway dependencies and will keep your layers cleanly segregated.

Another question that frequently comes up while discussing purity of the application layers is how to handle so-called *cross-cutting concerns*. The term refers to a need to have a higher layer perform the work which belongs to a lower layer.

Let's consider a snippet from our hypothetical banking system from the earlier:

```
<code>
interface Domain {
  commandModel : CommandModel;
  queryModel : QueryModel;
};
interface BankingServices {

  deposit(
    domain : Domain,
    toAccountNumber : number,
    amount : number
  ) : { toAccount : AccountAggregate };

  …

};
const myBankingServices : BankingServices = {
  deposit(
    domain : Domain,
    toAccountNumber: number,
    amount : number
  ) : { toAccount : AccountAggregate } {
    let { transactionId } =
      domain.commandModel.recordTransaction<DepositTransactionArgs>(
        TransactionType.DEPOSIT,
        { toAccountNumber : toAccountNumber }
      );
    domain.commandModel.recordLedgerEntry(
      toAccountNumber,
      amount,
      transactionId
    );
    return {
      toAccount : domain.queryModel.getAccount( toAccountNumber )
    };
  },

  …

}
</code>
```

Now, let's imagine that we want to log every call to any of the Banking Services, and also to begin a new database transaction at the beginning of each service, commit it at the end, and roll it back if the service crashes. Let's have a look at what happens to the code in the deposit() method if we do this.

First, our business logic will have to access the mechanisms controlling transactions and logging. Usually, those are implemented as a part of the Infrastructure layer, which is not available to our business logic yet. To address this, we must come up with a way to create a limited access to the Infrastructure, to be consumed by our business logic. Here is how we can do this cleanly:

```
<code>
interface Logger {
  write(msg: string, err? : Error ): void;
}
interface TransactionManager {
  beginTransaction() : void;
  commitTransaction() : void;
  rollbackTransaction() : void;
}
interface Infrastructure {
  transactions : TransactionManager;
  logger : Logger;
}
interface Domain {
  commandModel : CommandModel;
  queryModel : QueryModel;
  infrastructure : Infrastructure;
};
</code>
```

Now we have a clean controlled way to access a subset of infrastructure's features from our business logic.

Next, let's add transactions and logging to the deposit() method.

```
<code>
deposit(
  domain : Domain,
  toAccountNumber: number,
  amount : number
) : { toAccount : AccountAggregate } {
  domain.infrastructure.logger.write( `making deposit - begin` );
  domain.infrastructure.transactions.beginTransaction();
  try {
    let { transactionId } =
      domain.commandModel.recordTransaction<DepositTransactionArgs>(
        TransactionType.DEPOSIT,
        { toAccountNumber : toAccountNumber }
      );
    domain.commandModel.recordLedgerEntry(
      toAccountNumber,
      amount,
      transactionId
    );
    let result : { toAccount : AccountAggregate } = {
      toAccount : domain.queryModel.getAccount( toAccountNumber )
    };
    domain.infrastructure.transactions.commitTransaction();
    return result;
  }
  catch( err ) {
    domain.infrastructure. logger.write( `making deposit - failed`, err );
    domain.infrastructure.transactions.rollbackTransaction();
    return null;
  }
  finally {
    domain.infrastructure.logger.write( `making deposit - end` );
  }
}
</code>
```

We just did what many software developers would have done without thinking twice: we simply added logging and transaction handling directly to the deposit() method. By doing this, we significantly increased the size of the code. The code is now also much harder to read because the business logic is now interspersed with logging and transaction code which belongs to a lower layer! Worse, we now have a confusion between banking "transactions" and database "transactions"; they represent terminology of different domains which are now intertwined in our code.

Now imagine what happens once we start adding security, telemetry, and other *cross-cutting concerns* that just don't belong. The boilerplate code we add to our business logic over time reduces the *signal-to-noise ratio*, meaning it becomes increasingly hard to read and understand the business logic, as the increasingly larger portion of the business logic has literally nothing to do with the business.

Luckily, there is a better way. We can create a universal "proxy" implementation for a service, suitable for any service call, and use it for all service calls in our code. The implementation would differ from one language to another, but it is possible to implement this pattern in practically any modern programming language. Here is one of the most simplistic ways of doing it in TypeScript. First, we standardize on the signature of any service method:

```
<code>
interface Services {
  [method: string]: Function;
};

interface MethodArgs {
}

interface MethodResult {
}

type ServiceMethod<A extends MethodArgs, R extends MethodResult> =
  (domain: Domain, args: A) => R;
</code>
```

With this, our BankingServices interface may look as follows:

```
<code>
interface OpenAccountArgs extends MethodArgs {
};

interface OpenAccountResult extends MethodResult {
  newAccount: AccountAggregate;
};

interface DepositArgs extends MethodArgs {
  toAccountNumber: number;
  amount: number;
};

interface DepositResult extends MethodResult {
  toAccount: AccountAggregate;
};

interface WithdrawalArgs extends MethodArgs {
  fromAccountNumber: number;
```

```
    amount: number;
};

interface WithdrawalResult extends MethodResult {
  fromAccount: AccountAggregate;
};

interface TransferArgs extends MethodArgs {
  fromAccountNumber: number;
  toAccountNumber: number;
  amount: number;
};

interface TransferResult extends MethodResult {
  toAccount: AccountAggregate;
  fromAccount: AccountAggregate;
};

interface BankingServices extends Services {
  openAccount: ServiceMethod<OpenAccountArgs, OpenAccountResult>;
  deposit: ServiceMethod<DepositArgs, DepositResult>;
  withdraw: ServiceMethod<WithdrawalArgs, WithdrawalResult>;
  transfer: ServiceMethod<TransactionArgs, TransferResult>;
};
```
</code>

Now, because all services now share the same method signature, we can create a universal proxy augmentSerices() which can wrap any services interface (not necessarily just BankingServices). Here is how:

<code>
```
const augmentServices = <T extends Services>(services: T): T => {
  let augmentedServices: Services = {};
  for(let methodName in services) {
    augmentedServices[methodName] =
      (domain: Domain, args: MethodArgs): MethodResult => {
        domain.infrastructure.logger.write( `entering ${methodName}` );
        domain.infrastructure.transactions.beginTransaction();
        try {
          let result = services[methodName](domain, args);
          domain.infrastructure.transactions.commitTransaction();
          return result;
        }
        catch( err ) {
          domain.infrastructure.logger.write(`failed in ${methodName}`, err );
          domain.infrastructure.transactions.rollbackTransaction();
          return null;
        }
        finally {
          domain.infrastructure.logger.write(`exiting ${methodName}`);
```

```
            }
        };
    }
    return augmentedServices as T;
};
</code>
```

Here, `augmentServices()` accepts any interface that extends Services, and automatically handles transactions and logging for it.

Finally, we create our implementation of `BankingServices` and wrap it with `augmentServices` to add the cross-cutting concerns to it:

```
<code>
  const myBankingServices = augmentServices<BankingServices>({

    openAccount(
      domain: Domain,
      args: OpenAccountArgs
    ): OpenAccountResult {
      let {accountNumber} = domain.commandModel.createAccount();
      return {
        newAccount: domain.queryModel.getAccount(accountNumber)
      };
    },

    deposit(
      domain: Domain,
      args: DepositArgs
    ): DepositResult {
      let {transactionId} =
        domain.commandModel.recordTransaction<DepositTransactionArgs>(
          TransactionType.DEPOSIT,
          {toAccountNumber: args.toAccountNumber}
        );
      domain.commandModel.recordLedgerEntry(
        args.toAccountNumber,
        args.amount,
        transactionId
      );
      return {
        toAccount: domain.queryModel.getAccount(args.toAccountNumber)
      };
    },

    withdraw(
      domain: Domain,
      args: WithdrawalArgs
    ): WithdrawalResult {
      let {transactionId} =
```

```
        domain.commandModel.recordTransaction<WithdrawalTransactionArgs>(
          TransactionType.WITHDRAWAL,
          {fromAccountNumber: args.fromAccountNumber}
        );
      domain.commandModel.recordLedgerEntry(
        args.fromAccountNumber,
        ( -args.amount ),
        transactionId
      );
      return {
        fromAccount: domain.queryModel.getAccount(args.fromAccountNumber)
      };
    },

    transfer(
      domain: Domain,
      args: TransferArgs
    ): TransferResult {
      let {transactionId} =
        domain.commandModel.recordTransaction<TransferTransactionArgs>(
          TransactionType.TRANSFER,
          {
            fromAccountNumber: args.fromAccountNumber,
            toAccountNumber: args.toAccountNumber
          },
        );
      domain.commandModel.recordLedgerEntry(
        args.fromAccountNumber,
        ( -args.amount ),
        transactionId
      );
      domain.commandModel.recordLedgerEntry(
        args.toAccountNumber,
        args.amount,
        transactionId
      );
      return {
        fromAccount: domain.queryModel.getAccount(args.fromAccountNumber),
        toAccount: domain.queryModel.getAccount(args.toAccountNumber)
      };
    }
  });
</code>
```

As you can see, the business logic in the implementation of BankingServices is back to "normal", free of any logging or transaction handling. Implementation of additional cross-cutting concerns (security, telemetry, etc.) could be easily added to augmentServices() to make it more useful, and to keep the business logic clean.

Keep in mind that `augmentServices()` is a part of the infrastructure layer, and must be imported by the business logic. You can make it even cleaner, import `augmentServices()` into the domain layer, and then expose it to the business logic as a part of the `Domain` interface. This way, your domain will have full control over which of the infrastructure's services are available to the business logic, and your Application layer will never import anything from the Infrastructure layer directly – which is how it should be in the ideal world.

<tldr>

Break your system into layers and keep them separate. Consider creating a domain-specific language (DSL) for the application layer, as a way to promote simplicity and separation. If using general-purpose language (GPL) for building the application layer, create a restrictive framework and a process to keep the application layer from intermingling with the layers below.
Do not allow cross-cutting concerns to penetrate your business logic. Use the proxy pattern to keep cross-cutting concerns where they belong.

https://anatoly.com/layering

</tldr>

CHAPTER 6
CODE COMPOSITION

> *I'm not concerned about all hell breaking loose, but that a PART of hell will break loose… it'll be much harder to detect.*
> *– George Carlin*

As architect, you must create coding guidelines for other developers and for yourself to follow. Not only you must know how to properly compose the code, but you must be able to mentor the team. In this chapter, we will cover the five famous principles of code composition known as SOLID. Those principles apply at different levels – from splitting your code into modules, to creating class hierarchies, to breaking your code into microservices and designing APIs.

SOLID is not a full-encompassing set of principles. There are more, many more. These are arguably the most widely known. However, if you are hungry for more (as you should be), then consider the recommended reading materials listed in Appendix II.

The SOLID principles are:

- The **S**ingle Responsibility Principle (SRP)
- The **O**pen-Closed Principle (OCP)
- The **L**iskov Substitution Principle (LSP)
- The **I**nterface Segregation Principle (ISP)
- The **D**ependency Inversion Principle (DIP)

I have to warn you – those are principles, not patterns. They don't not tell you how to create a good architecture. But they warn you if you are veering off course, into uncharted shark-infested waters of spaghetti designs. On my part, I will do my best to illustrate the principles, and to equip you with the most common solutions as we go.

The Single Responsibility Principle (SRP). Originally this principle was formulated as "*A module should have one, and only one, reason to change*". The "module" can be loosely interpreted as a "component" – a class, a function, an interface, a source file, etc. – depending on which units of code composition you are working on. This principle is frequently interpreted as *a component should serve one, and only one purpose*. While this is a good principle on its own, this is *not* what the Single Responsibility Principle is about. To reach clarity, I suggest rephrasing the original SRP language as follows: *a component should have one, and only one source of change*. Here, the "*source of change*" is typically a person or a team responsible for business specifications – in other words, *those who ask for changes*.

The logic behind this is fairly straightforward. Imagine that you are building an e-commerce system, and your checkout process is represented by a single function that handles payment, notifies the customer, and fulfils the order:

```
<code>
const checkout = (
    cc : CardInformation,
    totalAmount : number,
    shippingAddress : StreetAddress,
    emailAddress : string,
    phoneNumber : string,
    productId : string,
    quantity : number
) : void => {
    chargeCard( cc, totalAmount );
    sendConfirmationEmail( emailAddress );
    sendConfirmationSMS( phoneNumber );
    let parcel = packParcel( productId, quantity );
    let trackingNumber = printShippingLabel( parcel, shippingAddress );
    orderPickup( trackingNumber );
};
</code>
```

The requirements for payment handling are driven by your accounting team, the requirements for customer notifications come from the marketing team, and packing and shipping are owned by the fulfillment team. As time goes by, each of the three teams evolve their own set of requirements, tearing your single checkout() function apart.

With that in mind, you are much better off by breaking the checkout() function into three independent ones, for example:

```
<code>
const pay = ( // satisfies accounting requirements
  cc : CardInformation,
  totalAmount : number
) : void => {
  chargeCard( cc, totalAmount );
};

const notify = ( // satisfies marketing requirements
  emailAddress : string,
  phoneNumber : string
) : void => {
  sendConfirmationEmail( emailAddress );
  sendConfirmationSMS( phoneNumber );
};

const fulfill = ( // satisfies fulfillment requirements
  productId : string,
  quantity : number,
  shippingAddress : StreetAddress
) : void => {
  let parcel = packParcel( productId, quantity );
  let trackingNumber = printShippingLabel( parcel, shippingAddress );
  orderPickup( trackingNumber );
};

const checkout = (
  cc : CardInformation,
  totalAmount : number,
  shippingAddress : StreetAddress,
  emailAddress : string,
  phoneNumber : string,
  productId : string,
  quantity : number
) : void => {
  // work for accounting
  pay( cc, totalAmount );
  // work for marketing
  notify( emailAddress, phoneNumber );
  // work for fulfillment
  fulfill( productId, quantity, shippingAddress );
};
</code>
```

Now, you can place functions pay(), notify() and fulfill() into separate modules, and have them maintained independently. This allows you to implement the ever-changing and expanding requirements coming from the three product teams in their own respective places.

Naturally, in an early-stage startup, you may have the same person defining all of the above aspects – and you must use your imagination and experience to anticipate the growth of the company through your architecture.

Violation of the Single Responsibility Principle leads to complex and unreliable merges of changes. When the code is checked in, you should rarely go through diffing the source code. If you are diffing the code on merges on regular basis, then your architecture violates the Single Responsibility Principle. But complex and risky code merges is only a beginning. Eventually, violating the SRP principle leads to a situation when *shared code can no longer be shared*. For instance, let's look at the checkout functionality. Let's say you have a function `getOrderTotal()` which returns the total amount for the order. Then it turns out that for accounting purposes, you must return the amount before tax, but the end user must see the amount with tax included. Changing the function is not an option, because it is shared, and fixing it for one context will break it for another. This is because this function violates the Single Responsibility Principle. We should have had three functions from the very beginning: `getOrderTotalBeforeTax()`, `getOrderTax()`, and `getOrderTotalToDisplay()`. The first two functions are responsible for retrieving the factual information that is universally useful, and the third function is used specifically for displaying the information to an end user.

<important>

The Single Responsibility Principle helps you redirect the streams of future changes from different sources into their own modules, one module per source. This helps to avoid conflicts on code merges and keeps shared code shareable despite the potentially breaking changes.

</important>

The Open-Closed Principle (OCP) says: "*A software artifact[17] should be open for extension but closed for modification*". To make things simpler, I'd like to re-phrase it as "*Extending the behavior of a software artifact should not require modification of the original code of that artifact.*" This principle pushes us toward anticipating the future and constructing our software in an extensible way. The principle by itself does not tell us how. If adding new functionality causes significant changes in the existing software, then we know we didn't do a good job following the Open-Closed Principle.

Let's consider an example. We have an interface that defines any rectangular shape as follows:

```
<code>
class  Rectangle {
  width : number;
  height : number;
}
</code>
```

Now, we are asked to build a calculator that computes the total area of multiple rectangles:

```
<code>
const computeTotalArea = ( shapes : Rectangle[] ) : number => {
  let area : number = 0;
  for( let shape of shapes ) {
    area += ( shape.width * shape.height );
  }
  return area;
};
</code>
```

Looks ok? Let's say we accept the above solution. A few months later, we are asked to add handling of circles into the mix.

---

[17] The *software artifact* could be a class, a module, a function, etc.

Without much thinking, we could do it this way:

```
<code>
enum ShapeType {
  RECTANGLE, CIRCLE
}
abstract class Shape {
  type : ShapeType;
}
class Rectangle extends Shape {
  type : ShapeType.RECTANGLE;
  width : number;
  height : number;
}
class Circle extends Shape {
  type : ShapeType.CIRCLE;
  radius : number;
}
const computeTotalArea = ( shapes : Shape[] ) : number => {
  let area : number = 0;
  for( let shape of shapes ) {
    switch( shape.type ) {
      case ShapeType.RECTANGLE: {
        let rect = shape as Rectangle;
        area += ( rect.width * rect.height );
        break;
      }
      case ShapeType.CIRCLE: {
        let circ = shape as Circle;
        area += ( circ.radius * circ.radius * Math.PI );
        break;
      }
      default:
        throw new Error(`Unsupported shape.type=${shape.type}`);
    }
  }
  return area;
};
</code>
```

This will work – but – we are getting on the slippery path where each additional shape type will force us to change the implementation of computeTotalArea(). This violates the Open-Closed Principle, which demands that alteration of behavior is achieved through *extending* the code, without *changing* it.

Here is an example of how this can be fixed:

```
<code>
abstract class Shape {
  abstract computeArea() : number;
}

class Rectangle extend Shape {
  width : number;
  height : number;
  computeArea() : number {
    return ( this.width * this.height );
  }
}

class Circle extends Shape {
  radius : number;
  computeArea() : number {
    return ( this.radius * this.radius * Math.PI );
  }
}

const computeTotalArea = ( shapes : Shape[] ) : number => {
  let area : number = 0;
  for( let shape of shapes ) {
    area += shape.computeArea();
  }
  return area;
};
</code>
```

Now, you can add any number of shapes without modifying computeTotalArea(). Place each shape implementation in its own module (file) to further insulate the logic of computeTotalArea() from the implementations of shape-specific classes.

Remember that this is just an example, and not a universal solution to fix violations of the Open-Closed Principle. You may have to get creative when facing this problem.

I am frequently asked how one can anticipate the need for a change, to create the correct design in the first place. Generally, it comes with experience. But still, no one is able to anticipate all possible changes coming your way, and preparing for hypothetical changes which may never come is likely to make your code more complex than it should be. It's not worth the trouble. However, once you see that a change forces you to violate OCP, you must immediately refactor your code to fix the problem. Left unattended, the problem gets bigger over time, becoming much harder to fix as the code base grows.

<important>
The Open-Closed Principle helps detect a need for refactoring early, while it is still relatively inexpensive. Your programing language and tooling must support efficient refactoring for this process to be less painful.
</important>

The Liskov Substitution Principle (LSP). When I read the original description of the principle by Barbara Liskov, I went through it several times, and I still had no idea what to do with it… not until I read the explanation. See for yourself: *"If for each object O1 of type S there is an object O2 of type T such that for all programs P defined in terms of T, the behavior of P is unchanged when O1 is substituted for O2 then S is a subtype of T"*. What do you think of it?

This principle is about the proper use of inheritance in OOP. Those of you using functional programming, or those who avoid using inheritance in OOP, are "automatically" in the clear. For those of you who use inheritance, please read on.

If you find the language of LSP complex or confusing, then you are not alone. Let me rephrase it for you: *"The behavior of any piece of code that uses the base class should not change if the base class is substituted with a derived class"*, or *"a reference to the base class should be replaceable with a derived class without affecting the behavior"*. Essentially, it is a readability test for your class hierarchy.

Let's consider this example, which implements calculation of an area for rectangular or square geometric shapes:

<code>
```
class Rectangle {
  width: number;
  height: number;
  constructor() {
    this.width = 0;
    this.height = 0;
  }
  setWidth( width : number ) : void {
    this.width = width;
```
</code>

```
  }
  setHeight( height : number ) : void {
    this.height = height;
  }
  getArea() : number {
    return this.width * this.height;
  }
}
class Square extends Rectangle {
  constructor() {
    super();
    this.width = this.height = 0;
  }
  // override to make it a square
  setWidth( width : number ) : void {
    this.width = this.height = width;
  }
  // override to make it a square
  setHeight( height : number ) : void {
    this.width = this.height = height;
  }
}
```
</code>

In this example, we have a class Rectangle that has width and height properties to specify the dimensions, and class Square that inherits from Rectangle and modifies the setter methods to maintain the square aspect ratio.

Now, let's consider this piece of code:

<code>
```
let rc : Rectangle

// test A
rc = new Rectangle();
rc.setWidth( 5 );
rc.setHeight( 10 );
console.log( rc.getArea() ); // prints 50

// test B
rc = new Square();
rc.setWidth( 5 );
rc.setHeight( 10 );
console.log( rc.getArea() ); // prints 100
```
</code>

In both tests A and B, we use the same variable rc of type Rectangle, but in test B its behavior is unexpected for a rectangle.

Why is it important, you may wonder? You may further argue that you can see the actual classes instantiated in the tests A and B respectively, and they give you a clear hint at how to predict the behavior of the code. Consider the slightly modified version of the same code:

```
const test = ( rc : Rectangle ) : void => {
  rc.setWidth( 5 );
  rc.setHeight( 10 );
  console.log( rc.getArea() ); // prints what???
};

// test A
test( new Rectangle() );

// test B
test( new Square() );
```

Now, the behavior of function `test()` is totally unpredictable. It is impossible to guess what results it will produce, without analyzing each invocation of the function, of which there could be hundreds or thousands.

Now let's revisit the simplified language of the Liskov principle: "*a reference to the base class should be replaceable with a derived class without affecting the behavior*". In our example, substituting the base class Rectangle with a derived class Square changes the behavior of function `test()`, making the function's behavior unpredictable. Our class hierarchy violates the LSP principle, and therefore our hierarchy is incorrect[18].

If you are wondering how to fix this, consider the following:

```
abstract class Shape {
  abstract getArea() : number;
}

class Rectangle extends Shape {
  width: number;
  height: number;
  constructor() {
    super();
    this.width = 0;
    this.height = 0;
```

---

[18] To be clear, our class hierarchy is perfectly valid syntactically, but is invalid from the practical point of view guarded by the Liskov principle.

```
    }
    setWidth( width : number ) : void {
      this.width = width;
    }
    setHeight( height : number ) : void {
      this.height = height;
    }
    // override
    getArea() : number {
      return this.width * this.height;
    }
  }
  class Square extends Shape {
    side: number;
    constructor() {
      super();
      this.side = 0;
    }
    setSide( side : number ) : void {
      this.side = side;
    }
    // override
    getArea() : number {
      return this.side * this.side;
    }
  }
</code>
```

Notice this structure prevents us from whiting the code like this:

```
<code>
  const test = ( sh : Shape ) : void => {
    sh.setWidth( 5 ); // compile time error
    sh.setHeight( 10 ); // compile time error
    console.log( sh.getArea() );
  };
  // test A
  test( new Rectangle() );

  // test B
  test( new Square() );
</code>
```

Now we can only use the sh argument to apply the methods common to all kinds of shape, such as getArea() but not setWidth() and setHeight() which are specific to rectangle only, while square supports setSide() instead.

Another logical improvement in this particular case is to move the initialization parameters into constructors, which are specific to each individual class, like this:

```
abstract class Shape {
  abstract getArea() : number;
}
class Rectangle extends Shape {
  width: number;
  height: number;
  constructor( width : number, height : number ) {
    super()
    this.width = width;
    this.height = height;
  }
  // override
  getArea() : number {
    return this.width * this.height;
  }
}
class Square extends Shape {
  side: number;
  constructor( side : number ) {
    super()
    this.side = side;
  }
  // override
  getArea() : number {
    return this.side * this.side;
  }
}
```

Now our test code looks like this:

```
const test = ( sh : Shape ) : void => {
  console.log( sh.getArea() );
};

// test A
test( new Rectangle(5,10) );

// test B
test( new Square(10) );
```

Does it look perfect now? Maybe, but I'd like to take it just a little bit further. In our example and in many other cases, it may become apparent that the inheritance of classes is completely necessary. For instance, our example can be rewritten using interfaces and without any class inheritance:

```
<code>
interface Shape {
  getArea() : number;
}
class Rectangle implements Shape {
  width: number;
  height: number;
  constructor( width : number, height : number ) {
    this.width = width;
    this.height = height;
  }
  // implements Shape
  getArea() : number {
    return this.width * this.height;
  }
}
class Square implements Shape {
  side: number;
  constructor( side : number ) {
    this.side = side;
  }
  // implements Shape
  getArea() : number {
    return this.side * this.side;
  }
}
</code>
```

Looks trivial? Great, start using it right away.

<important>

The Liskov Substitution Principle guards against creating the code that will be hard to understand by simply reading it. Eliminating class inheritance ensures 100% compliance with Liskov Principle. You should have a very good justification for using inheritance in the first place.

</important>

\

The Interface Segregation Principle (ISP) states that *no client should be forced to depend on methods it does not use.* Sounds obvious? Let's take a closer look.

Consider an e-commerce system that sells products. Each product can be purchased, and each product can be shipped to a customer. There is a variety of products that the system sells, so we make them all compliant with the same contract. The first knee-jerk reaction is to define it like this:

\<code>
```
interface Product {
  purchase() : void;
  ship() : void;
}

const checkout = ( p : Product ) : boolean => {
  p.purchase();
  return true;
};

const delivery = ( p : Product ) : boolean => {
  p.ship();
  return true;
};
```
\</code>

Notice anything wrong with this implementation? It clearly violates the Interface Segregation Principle. The code executing at the checkout time depends on implementing the entire product. As such, it depends on the `ship()` method which is not called at checkout time but must be included because the `Product` interface demands so. Similar problem with the delivery code, which depends on the `purchase()` method without calling it. Those dependencies require you to rebuild and redeploy your delivery services when checkout code changes, and vice versa. This leads to monolithic implementation which must be built and deployed all at once. This may not be a problem in a small project, but in a larger system it will invariably lead to slow rebuilds, lengthy deploys, and excessive hardware requirements. It will also hamper your ability to deliver stable software releases more often.

A solution is in breaking your interfaces into smaller ones, driven not by the object that implements the interface, but by the code that consumes the interface. Our first step is to define the interfaces like this:

```
<code>
interface Checkout {
  purchase() : void;
}

interface Delivery {
  ship() : void;
}

const checkout = ( c : Checkout ) : boolean => {
  c.purchase();
  return true;
};

const deliver = ( d : Delivery ) : boolean => {
  d.ship();
  return true;
};
</code>
```

Now, how shall we define the product contract? Again, the knee-jerk reaction could be to do something like this:

```
<code>
class Product implements Checkout, Delivery {
  constructor() { … }
  purchase() : void { … }
  ship() : void { … }
}
</code>
```

But with this implementation, the entire Product class will be always required whenever we use Checkout or Delivery interfaces independently, still violating the Interface Segregation Principle. The correct solution may push us further away from the traditional OOP, into the land of functional programming – because we just realized that typical OOP coupling of data with all the behaviors is not always a good idea.

If we do things right, we may end up with something like this:

```
<code>
class ProductData {

  …
}
class ProductCheckoutService implements Checkout {
  data : ProductData;
  constructor( data : ProductData ) { this.data = data; }
  purchase() : void { … }
}
class ProductDeliveryService implements Delivery {
  data : ProductData;
  constructor( data : ProductData ) { this.data = data; }
  ship() : void { … }
}
</code>
```

Now we have the code of checkout and fulfillment services in separate classes, which can be placed each in their own source file, and compiled/deployed/loaded independently.

<important>

The Interface Segregation Principle guards again creation of monolithic applications with intertwined module dependencies. Monolithic applications are harder and slower to build, and sluggish to start.

</important>

The Dependency Inversion Principle (DIP) states that your *higher-level implementation should never depend on a lower-level implementation, but rather on an abstraction of that lower-level implementation.*

We briefly touched on Dependency Inversion while discussing interfaces and layering earlier, but now we will generalize it for a more widespread use. In general, when one source code module imports another, it should only import interfaces, and never concrete implementations. This comes naturally to some older programming languages like C/C++ in which "header files" are used for declaration purposes only, and normally contain no concrete code. In more contemporary languages, you are not forced into this paradigm, but you can elect to split your code into multiple source files as you see fit.

Let's take the logger implementation from the programming language example, from the earlier in the book, and arrange it correctly across several source files to avoid violating the Dependency Inversion Principle.

Module `logger-defs` contains contract definitions for logging:

```
// module logger-defs.ts

export interface Logger {
  log( value : string ) : void;
};
```

Module `logger-impl` contains implementation of a logger, and it depends only on contract definitions for logging:

```
// module logger-impl.ts

import { Logger } from './logger-defs';

export const myLogger : Logger = {
  log( value : string ) : void {
    console.log( `*** ${ value }` );
  }
};
```

Module `foo` contains the application logic, and it depends only on contract definitions for logging – and not on the specific logging implementation:

```
// module foo.ts

import { Logger } from './logger-defs';

export const foo = ( logger : Logger ) : void => {
  logger.log( `entered function foo` );
};
```

Why bother with such complexity? Imagine that your function foo() can be used both in the browser and on the server side. The two environments are likely to have different loggers. With Dependency Inversion, foo() receives an abstraction of a logger in a form of its interface, passed as a parameter. Foo() is unaware of any concrete implementation of the logger and therefore does not have to be changed, regardless of where it is be running.

In real life, we'll have many interfaces to pass as arguments, besides the logger – ideally, all underlying services should be implemented in a similar way. This may lead to significant bloat of the parameter list. It can be avoided by collecting all dependencies in a single Environment interface:

```
// module environment-defs.ts

import { Logger } from './logger-defs';

export interface Environment {
  logger : Logger;
  // other dependencies go here
}
```

Now, let's create module bar which replaces foo from the previous example:

```
// module bar.ts

import {Environment} from './environment-defs';

export const bar = ( env : Environment ) : void => {
  env.logger.log( `entered function bar` );
};
```

All environmental dependencies are now available to foo() via the single environment argument.

You may notice that we already used this approach, without explaining it, when discussing segregation of layers. There, we had Domain and Infrastructure interfaces as abstract representations of Domain and Infrastructure layers, respectively, to the higher-level Application layer.

The method of passing an abstraction (an interface, or an API endpoint) as a parameter to either a function or to a class via its constructor is commonly known as *Dependency Injection (DI) pattern*. This is not the only method of becoming compliant with Dependency Inversion Principle, but it is by far the most widespread.

As you may realize, the concrete implementation of your interfaces would have to be placed somewhere. You may further decouple your code from specifying concrete implementations of your interfaces by instantiating your classes dynamically based on a configuration stored in a file. This way, you can launch your application and make it use different implementations of your interfaces depending on the deployment environment. For instance, you may have different implementations of a Logger in development vs test vs production environments, simply by supplying different configuration files. Such approach is known as *Inversion of Control (IoC)*. The name reflects the fact that your code no longer fully controls the behavior of your application, and that control is being delegated to an external configuration file, or to a framework[19].

So now we know how to inject a dependency by passing an interface as a parameter. But what if your code must create an arbitrary number of objects? For instance, consider building a painting functionality which draws various shapes on the screen. The type of the shape to draw is determined by time. You don't want to have a dependency on concrete implementations of the specific shapes, but there has to be a new statement somewhere instantiating concrete shapes. How would you code it?

For this, we combine Dependency Injection with another very popular technique called the *Factory Pattern*. The idea behind is simple: move creation of concrete objects to a separate class (the Factory), and then decouple from the factory using Dependency Injection. Here is what it looks like.

First, let's define all interfaces in module shapes-defs:

```
<code>
// module shapes-defs.ts
export interface Canvas {
  ...
}
```

---

[19] There are many frameworks that implement IoC. A good example from Java world is Spring. I am not a big fan of such frameworks, because they tend to intertwine with your code, growing through it like a tumor, eventually becoming irreplaceable. Writing your own code to read a configuration file and to dynamically instantiate your classes is trivial.

```
export interface Shape {
  draw( canvas : Canvas, x : number, y : number ) : void;
}
export interface ShapeFactory {
  createShape( time : Date ) : Shape;
}
```
</code>

This defines the contracts for `Shape` and for `ShapeFactory`. `Shape` can draw itself, and `ShapeFactory` can create new shapes based on time.

Next, we write our code which draws the shapes over time, in module `draw`:

<code>
```
// module draw.ts

import { Canvas, Shape, ShapeFactory } from './shapes-def';

const draw = ( shapeFactory : ShapeFactory, canvas : Canvas ) : void => {
  const drawSingleShape = () => {
    let shape = shapeFactory.createShape( new Date() );
    shape.draw( canvas, Math.random() * 100, Math.random() * 100 );
  };
  for( let i = 0; i < 100; i++ ) {
    setTimeout( drawSingleShape, i * 1000 );
  }
};
```
</code>

Now, our code is completely independent from the concrete implementations of both `Shape` and `ShapeFactory`. The latter decides which shape to create, based on the time value passed to it, and each shape has its own way of drawing itself.

<important>

The Dependency Inversion Principle pushes you toward creating abstractions (usually interfaces) for all your software components. This makes it easy to substitute implementations of those components without changing the rest of your code base. The most common patterns for abstracting components are Dependency Injection and Factory. Your code may delegate creation of concrete implementation instances for your abstractions to a configuration file by applying the Inversion of Control pattern.

</important>

To wrap up the discussion on SOLID principles, there is one more piece of advice. You cannot catch all SOLID violations at design time; many will surface during the coding cycle. You will have to keep your team on high alert, detect SOLID violations early, and refactor the code mercilessly, every time a violation is detected. Don't just label those cases as "technical debt" to be handled later, because the more code is written against an improperly composed structure, the harder it is to refactor. Your technical debt increases with each line of code written thereafter, unless you nip the problem in the bud right away.

<tldr>

Apply SOLID principles to test if your architecture is compliant. Mentor your team to fully understand SOLID; those principles apply to almost everything in the software development. Refactor the code at the earliest signs of violation of any of the SOLID principles.

https://anatoly.com/code-composition

</tldr>

CHAPTER 7
LATENCY

May the forces of evil become confused on the way to your house.
– George Carlin

In 2014, I was putting together a loyalty program for a major water brand. Each pack of bottled water had an insert with a unique link, and the customers could open the link on their phone, register, and earn points. Later, the accumulated points could be exchanged for various rewards.

The scale of the system was massive – about 3.5 billion bottles of water went through the program just in the first 3 months. The traffic was very spiky, and most users were new to the system, with no data cached on their mobile phones yet. Our telemetry showed that 100% of the users who had to wait for over 7 seconds were abandoning the program, and 50% of those who had to wait for over 5 seconds were also bailing out. Protecting their reputation, the brand set the latency threshold for us at 3 seconds. That was tough, considering how graphics-heavy our web app was, how spiky the traffic turned out to be, and generally low performance of wireless networks in some parts of the country. After trimming everything down, we just barely squeezed our average response time below the required 3 seconds, right before the launch date, and went live with the system.

All was going well for a couple of months. Then a few smart dudes found a way to game the system by claiming the same reward URL concurrently from multiple devices. It was easy to fix, took us a few hours, and we pushed the update out. All went well until the typical grocery store shopping spike around 5 pm. Turned out that our fix created a database contention, which pushed our first page load time well into the 3-6 second territory. The problem could not be easily solvable with additional hardware, and we had to roll the fix back, and lived with the bug for another week, while working on a far more involving alternative solution.

That's the thing about latency – you don't know when and how it will hit you. It creeps up at the most unfortunate time, from seemingly benign software updates.

While latency should be included into your normal regression testing cycle to catch the problems early, before they hit your production system, there are also a few safeguards which you can build into your architecture early on – and that's what we will be focusing on in this chapter.

While many factors contribute to latency, I will coarsely classify them by the three main categories: *Client Latency*, *Network Latency*, and *Server Latency*.

Client Latency can be defined as a *delay caused by the execution of client-side code* (usually JavaScript code in the browser, or native code in mobile apps). Client latency can be reduced by:

- Using light-weight reactive frameworks like React/Redux, instead of the heavier frameworks of the past.

- Minifying your JavaScript code.

- Embracing asynchronicity, i.e., using the time spent on waiting for completion of network requests to perform useful computations in the background.

- Building a single-page app, to eliminate frequent page reloads. Each page load leads to re-initialization of the entire JavaScript codebase, which is time-consuming. Conversely, single-page app loads all the assets once, and rely on AJAX calls to the server to operate. In single-page apps, rendering of HTML typically occurs within the browser, instead of having the HTML rendered by the server and then delivered to the client.

- Perform CPU-intensive operations on the server side, especially for the applications targeting mobile devices.

Network Latency can be defined as a *delay caused by transmissions of data between the server and the client*. Such delays can be caused by (a) large number of transmissions between the client and the server while loading the first page, or in response to end user's actions, (b) slow handshake at the beginning of each network transmission, especially over encrypted connections, (c) slow connection speed, (d) by needing to transfer large amounts of data, and (e) by HTTP redirects. Generally, the more connections you have, and the more data you transfer over those connections, the higher the total network latency. Network latency can be reduced by these measures:

- Bundle scripts in as few files as possible, frequently achieved by using Webpack or similar script packaging utilities (browser only). Minify all the scripts.

- Bundle style sheets in as few files as possible.

- For responsive designs, and for mobile apps designed for multiple device form factors, resize images dynamically to be just of the right size. Use a coarse size grid to improve caching; for instance, always round both width and height of an image up to the next number divisible by 10 and clip the edges to the desired size using CSS. Consider third-party services for image resizing such as ImgIX or Cloudinary.

- Service all static resources via a Content Delivery Network (CDN)[20].

- Minimize the number of calls to your API endpoints. Consider designing the API to allow an arbitrary number of functions to be called in a single network roundtrip[21].

- Consider the possibility of making the API endpoints available geographically as close to the end user as possible. For instance, with Amazon Cloud, you can provision servers in multiple geographic regions, or have Amazon Lambda functions running in multiple geographic regions, or use of Amazon Lambda @Edge to get even closer to the end user.

- Leverage local storage to persist infrequently changing pieces of data.

Server Latency is defined as the *delay caused by the processing on the server side*. It includes *computational latency*, *database latency*, *synchronization latency*, and several other contributors. There are methods for reducing latency in those various categories, but there is one overarching principle which will help you keep the total server latency in check. It is based on a very simple idea: *not all the work of processing a user's request must be performed white the user is waiting*. When a request arrives from a user, it suffices to do just enough work to respond to the user (*synchronous* processing), and the rest of the work can be queued up and performed later (*asynchronous* processing). For instance, when a user places an order, it may suffice to generate a confirmation number, queue the order for future processing, and return the confirmation number to the user. The system can have an independent queue processor which picks up the pending orders from the queue and handles them.

---

[20] We will cover CDNs in further details in Chapter 11
[21] We will cover this method of API construction in Chapter 14

Generally, any user request can have two aspects, synchronous and asynchronous, as depicted here:

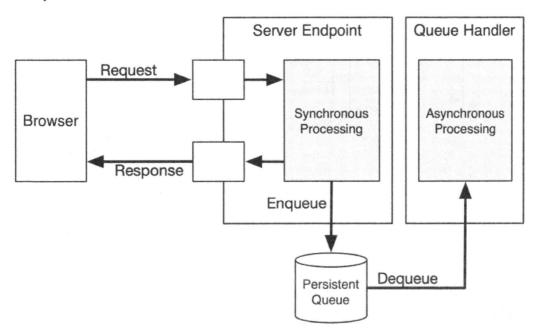

The Persistent Queue on the diagram can be implemented by using an off-the-shelf queueing or streaming implementation. For instance, in Amazon Cloud, you can build everything in a serverless manner: use SQS (queueing) or Kinesis (streaming) as a Persistent Queue, and implement asynchronous processing using AWS Lambda. As a vendor-neutral implementation, you can use Kafka to implement your persistent queues.

This diagram illustrates how this pattern functions in time:

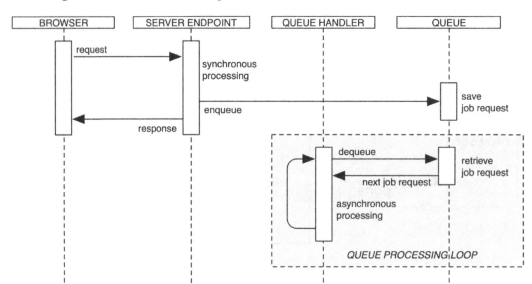

To make this pattern easily usable by the developers on your team, create a framework which only requires developers to write two snippets of code – one for synchronous processing, and one for asynchronous. The framework is responsible for invocation of those two snippets. For instance:

```
<code>
  interface Request {
    … // request received from the browser
  };

  interface Response {
    … // response to be sent to the browser
  };

  interface Context {
    … // execution context to pass from sync to async processing
  };

  interface Endpoint<Rq extends Request,Rs extends Response,C extends Context> {
    doSync( request : Rq ) : { response : Rs, context : C };
    doAsync( request : Rq, context : C ) : void;
  };
</code>
```

Your framework takes any concrete implementation of Endpoint, calls doSync() when a request from the UI is received by the endpoint, sends the response back, then enqueues the request and the context for asynchronous processing, and finally executes `doAsync()`. Developers must create their own versions of `Request`, `Response`, and `Context`, and implement the `Endpoint` interface. This way, you can completely shield your team from the complexity of handling asynchronicity and from the specifics of the underlying frameworks and services, allowing them to focus on the business logic.

Finally, don't forget about monitoring your system's latency on a continuous basis. There are several off-the-shelf services that can help, the most popular ones being New Relic and AppDynamics. If you are going serverless, you may need to do more manual work and manage your own telemetry feed.

<tldr>

Break your server-side processing into synchronous and asynchronous aspects. Make it easy for developers to code the asynchronous part by creating a framework. Optimize images and compress script and style assets. Use CDN for delivery of static assets. Collect telemetry to continuously monitor latency in your system.

https://anatoly.com/latency

</tldr>

CHAPTER 8
ERROR RECOVERY

If you try to fail, and succeed, which have you done?
– George Carlin

In this chapter, we will look closely at errors caused by the environment. Such errors are unavoidable, as they are not caused by "bugs" in the code which can be fixed. For instance, a lost network connection on your mobile device may cause your app to fail when attempting to contact the server. The most common remedy against such errors are retries: your code may either automatically retry the call to server, or it may prompt the user to confirm the retry attempt. In either case, there is a potential pitfall in such approach: you never know if your previous request never reached the server, or made it through and was processed but failed to transmit the result back. If you retry, you may process the same request more than once. Sometimes, it's ok. For instance, retrying a search for a product seems reasonably harmless. However, retrying a call to place an order may result in multiple identical order being placed. Speaking the tech lingo, your server-side implementation must be *idempotent* to make retries safe. Idempotent means that *your code can be executed multiple times with the same arguments, without changing the result or creating additional effects on the system or the environment, beyond the initial execution with those arguments.*

In practice, application code is rarely idempotent. Even a seemingly harmless search function, when applied multiple times, may skew analytical data, affect keyword usage stats, and create all sorts of unexpected damage.

Here is a design pattern which can make any server-side endpoint idempotent. First, we introduce Request Journal storage with records of the following structure:

```
<code>
interface RequestStorageRecord {
  requestId : string; // unique primary key
  receivedTimestamp : number;
  responseBody : any | null;
}
</code>
```

Then we put together the following process:

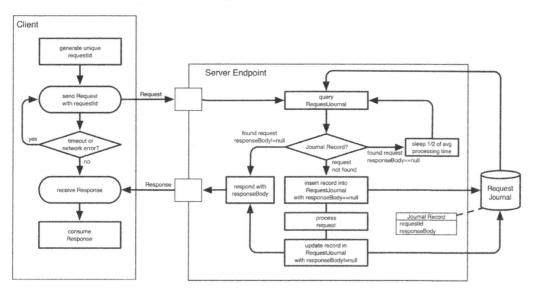

Here, we introduce Request Journal storage which records every inbound request. Requests are uniquely identified by `requestId`, which is generated by the client before sending an API call to the server. Once the request is received by the server but before it is processed, a new Request Journal record is created, with `requestId` from the received request alongside with the current time in `receivedTimestamp`, and `responseBody` is set to `null`. Once the request is fully processed, the journal record is updated with the `responseBody` containing the response, and then the response is sent back to the client. If the client times out or receives a network error, it retries the call with the same `requestId` as in the original request. The server-side code first queries Request Journal for the record with the received `requestId`. This leads to one of the three possible scenarios:

(a) No record with requested `requestId` is found in Request Journal. It means that the previous attempt did not make it through to the server, and it should be processed as described above, for the first time.

(b) The previous attempt to process the request has been already completed, i.e., `responseBody!=null`. In this case, we shall retrieve the recorded value of `responseBody` and return it back to the client without processing.

(c) The previous attempt to process the request is still in progress, i.e., `responseBody==null`. In this case, we wait until it is finished by periodically re-

reading the Journal Record and checking `responseBody`. Once we encounter `responseBody!=null`, we respond with it back to the client. We must have a built-in timeout for this, to avoid getting caught in an endless loop in case the processing crashes. The timeout is counted starting from the `receivedTimestamp` time, and should significantly exceed the anticipated processing time by the server, i.e.:

```
serverWaitTimeout = anticipatedServerProcessingTime * 10
```

Note this algorithm works properly only if the client performs retries sequentially, and only if the time interval between the calls made by the client exceeds the eventual consistency[22] promise of Request Journal database. It performs optimally if the time interval between the calls also significantly exceeds the anticipated processing time by the server. If written out as a formula:

```
timeBetweenRetries > max(
  eventualReadConsistencyGuarantee,
  anticipatedServerProcessingTime * 10
)
```

In real life, the algorithm can benefit from several additional refinements:

- If server-side processing crashes, it should still update the Request Journal with non-empty responseBody. Otherwise, a retry attempt will detect responseBody==null, assume that the request is still in progress (while it actually crashed), and wait until the timeout expires.

- The Request Journal can grow indefinitely, and quite fast. It is best to keep it clean of the old data. Some datastores like DynamoDB support Time to Live (TTL) setting for its records, which automatically deletes records from the store after a certain time threshold. The TTL value must significantly exceed the total time the client retries the call before reporting a permanent failure (in other words, while the client keeps sending the same requestId in its retry attempts.)

---

[22] Immediate read consistency means records written by one process are immediately available in their latest state to another process. Eventual read consistency means the records written by one process eventually become available to another process to read in their latest state, but no later than after a certain time interval passes by. Such time interval is called *read consistency guarantee*. Regardless of database engine, immediate consistency is a theoretical construct for any database accessed over a network, because no update query sent to the database reaches it immediately. Some of the database engines themselves also distinguish between immediate and eventual read consistency. For instance, DynamoDB has two types of reads – immediately consistent vs eventually consistent – and the former is pricier than the latter.

- The size of the Response can be quite large. Keep it in mind when choosing a storage solution for Request Journal. An alternative is to store responses in a cloud storage (like Amazon Simple Storage Service, aka S3), and record only a reference to the file in the cloud in the Request Journal. You can use this alternative approach for those requests that exceed the limits of the storage used for Request Journal. Keep in mind that cloud file operations are quite slow. Also, you need to plan for additional cleanup work, since the TTL-based cleanup of Request Journal records does not extend to the cloud storage.

- Create a telemetry feed to monitor retries. Frequent retry attempts are often caused by incorrectly set timeout values. Monitoring retries will help you fine-tune your timeout and retry settings.

- Retry algorithm on the client side can be improved by implementing exponential back-off. This means the time between retries should automatically increase with every attempt, up until a certain threshold is reached. This is to avoid overloading the system when an error persists for a duration of time.

- Retry algorithm can benefit from applying a circuit breaker pattern, i.e., by blocking access to the service entirely for a period of time, in case of consistent retry failures. For instance, once 10 attempts to access the service failed, stop all attempts to contact the service for the next 5 minutes – or display a Retry button for the customer to push manually.

Note that error handling described in this chapter works equally well with the errors caused by software bugs. Bugs are as unavoidable in large projects as environmental errors, and reliable error handling helps dealing with them just the same.

Embrace errors. Make your endpoints idempotent. Then use retries to recover.

https://anatoly.com/error-recovery

CHAPTER 9
LOGGING

We've added years to life, not life to years.
– George Carlin

Logging is one of the most useful tools for troubleshooting the system. Unfortunately, more often than not, it is added as an afterthought, which limits its usefulness. Logging strategy must be mapped out as a part of your architecture, because it affects the way it is engaged from the code.

Logs must be accessible from a *single access point*, for convenience. It is impractical, and sometimes impossible, to manually collect logs from production servers. A single access point could be implemented in many different ways. Some solutions store logs locally on each server and then ship log files asynchronously to a centralized location. This is a traditional approach, and it offers no support for serverless architectures, and rarely integrates client-side logging. Other solutions ship log entries immediately to a centralized location or upload to them to the cloud, where the logs are usually processed to make them searchable, for indexing purposes, and to collect statistics.

Logs must support *querying by context parameters* which are specific to your application domain. For instance, in an e-commerce system, we may want to query all log records that pertain to a certain user, or to a certain order, or to a certain time interval (or a combination of those). The hard part is getting the necessary context information embedded into every log entry since the code may not have access to the all context parameters when it writes new log entries. Worse, third-party components will never be able to add your domain-specific context to the log. For instance, you may be using an awesome library that charges credit cards, and the library may have good logging, but it will never be able to inject your application-specific user identity into the log, because it is completely unaware of it. The best solution for this is to maintain the necessary context in memory variables and create a log interceptor/writer which adds your context information to every log record created. Here is a crude illustration of how this might work for Node.js or in a browser[23]:

```
<code>
// implement log context
interface ILogContext {
  userId : string;
}
let globalLogContext : ILogContext = { userId : null };
const setLogContext = ( newLogContext : ILogContext ) : void => {
  globalLogContext = newLogContext;
};

// override default logging mechanism in Node.js or Browser
const defaultLogger = console.log;
console.log = ( ...args: any[] ) : void => {
  defaultLogger.apply(
    console,
    [ ...[`[userId=${globalLogContext.userId}]`], ...args ]
  );
};

...

// in the application code
...
setLogContext( { userId: `12345` } );
...
// there is no need to specify logging context in every write
console.log( `Hello` );
...
console.log( `World` );
...
setLogContext( { userId : null } );
</code>
```

This code snippet will produce log output like this:

```
<output>
[userId=12345] Hello
[userId=12345] World
</output>
```

The context value in the square brackets can be reliably parsed, and every message written to the log of your application now carries the context of its execution, event

---

[23] Similar mechanisms are available for practically all programming languages, supported either on the language level, or via popular libraries. For instance, log4j is one of the most popular logging frameworks in Java world.

if written by a third-party library. Now you can filter log records and retrieve only those that pertain to the specific user under investigation. Context may contain multiple values, allowing you to filter your logs by order numbers, products, and whatever else is useful. The code responsible for managing context can allow for various context parameters to be supplied at different times.

In multithreaded programs, a typical place to store log context is *thread local storage*, instead of a global variable. Every thread shall inherit the log context of the parent thread, and then maintain its own copy for the entire lifetime of the thread.

While logs are traditionally stored in files, it doesn't have to be that way. Logs entries could be sent to a streaming engine (e.g. Kafka or Kinesis), and then processed in a variety of way for further consumption. This enables you to collate log entries by context parameters, collect analytics, and send near-real time notifications when errors are detected.

To have the full picture for troubleshooting, it is invaluable to have *client-side logs* collected as well. More often than not, client-side logs remain locked in the browser or end up stored as log files on mobile devices, inaccessible for troubleshooting purposes. Yet, having the ability to "see" what happens on the client side significantly reduces the time and effort it takes to nail down production problems, especially those originating from the user interface.

There are two approaches to collecting client-side logs. One is to collect the logs in memory or in the browser's local storage, or in log files on mobile devices, and then ship the logs to the server with certain periodicity. This approach is taken by many third-party telemetry and logging SDKs for mobile apps. The drawback is usually that those logs end up in the cloud of the SDK's provider, and are not organically merged with server-side logs to clearly reflect the actual flow of events.

The other approach is to collect logs the same way but include the accumulated logging data with every request the client sends to the server in the course of the normal client/server chatter, and also independently if the client encounters an error, or if the client was not contacting the server for more than, say, 10 minutes, and has fresh logging data. This approach is very efficient, but requires that you have to build the log delivery mechanism directly into your client-server APIs.

Another feature which will save you lots of time during development is *shipping server-side logs to the client* alongside with the server's response. With this, developers can see both the client- and server-side logging in the browser or in the mobile device console. This feature can be turned off in production system but enabled in development and test. To make this work, add the respective functionality to your client-server APIs and wrap your API calls with a tiny framework which automatically prints server-side logging data once received by the client. Be careful not to re-send this data back to the server again, if you are shipping client-side logs to the server. If you are storing all responses to guarantee idempotence of error retries, then you may consider excluding logs from the stored responses to reduce storage requirements.

We will cover shipping of logs in further detail when we discuss APIs in Chapter 14.

The next extremely valuable feature of logging is *detecting crashes (exceptions)* and alerting someone when a crash occurs. It is usually wasteful to have someone scan through the logs manually, but you may want to be notified of a failure the very moment the system misbehaves. Sometimes, exceptions may be inadvertently "hidden" by the application logic, but a good coding style will have them printed every time an exception is thrown or caught. The system can send an email when this happens, or notify you with a Slack message, or sound an alarm via specialized alerting system like Pager Duty.

Finally, let's look at the common practice of assigning various *logging levels* (DEBUG, INFO, WARNING, ERROR or similar) to the logged content, to save on storage space once the system is stable. The tricky part is that the log is only as useful as the information stored in it. If you switch the detailed logging off in production by setting your logging level to ERROR, then it will contain no trace of the events which led to the error, because such information is usually tagged with either DEBUG or INFO level. My recommendation is to always log everything that comes from your code and use logging levels only to control the logging behavior of third-party libraries, as they get unnecessarily chatty from time to time. But whenever your team invests the time into adding a logging statement to the application, treasure it. One way of implementing this is to use a proprietary logging function everywhere throughout your code, which accepts no logging level as a parameter to individual logging calls. Your logging function then supplies the desired logging level internally. This way, you retain a fine-grained control over logging in third-party libraries, and always keep your own log entries.

Make logs accessible from a single point. Collect logs from both client and server. Support filtering of log entries by application-specific context parameters. Alert someone to crashes. Embrace chatty log levels. Shipping of client-side logs to the server helps troubleshooting. Shipping of server-side logs to the client at dev time speeds up development.

https://anatoly.com/logging

CHAPTER 10
REAL-TIME PROCESSING AND EVENT STREAMING

Those who dance are considered insane by those who cannot hear the music.

– George Carlin

Hard real-time (or more frequently near-real-time) solutions usually react to a stream of data that comes from sources other than human user input. Good examples of hard real-time systems are fly-by-wire systems in aircraft, autopilot solutions for self-driving vehicles, or network multimedia systems. Examples of near-real-time systems are ride-sharing applications (the likes of Uber and Lift), air traffic control systems, GPS navigation apps, various telemetry and real-time analytics solutions, or integration data feeds between applications.

The difference between hard- and near-real-time systems is primarily in the response time guarantee provided by the system for processing of incoming events. Hard real-time solutions require more than just a nicely done software architecture to function – they must have dedicated, fast and reliable communication channels, specialized dedicated hardware, etc. In this chapter, I will focus primarily on near-real-time architectures and will call them simply "real-time" going forward. Hard real-time systems may demand more from your architecture, going beyond the scope of this book.

One of the signature characteristics of a real-time system is the presence of one or several data streams that must be consumed (processed). For example, a GPS navigation app takes a continuous stream of car's coordinates, velocity and direction, to calculate its position on the map and its movement vector, and then to determine the optimal route to the destination. A more sophisticated navigation app may also accept another input stream with live road conditions and accident reports. A ride-sharing app adds a stream of ride requests, and a stream of events reflecting passengers starting and ending their rides.

If we attempt to process those streams of data synchronously, just like we process web requests, then we must have the server capacity sufficient for processing the highest spike in event traffic ever encountered. This might be sometimes possible with serverless architectures but is definitely cost-prohibitive for server-based infrastructures. You end up running way too many servers, most of them idling between the traffic spikes (i.e., most of the time). Auto-scaling solutions which automatically add servers to your installation are usually too slow to react to unpredictable traffic spikes; they scale reliably in response to variations in the sustained load, but not momentarily. A warm-up time of a server is too high for the system to retain its real-time characteristics. An attempt to immediately handle all events has other significant risks: you may easily exceed the number of network connections allowed, or you may quickly deplete the pool of database connections.

To address these problems, a number of streaming frameworks have sprouted in recent years. In this book, we will consider the two most representative ones: *Apache Kafka* and *Amazon Kinesis*.

Let's start with the diagram below, depicting how a streaming framework fits into the architecture of a hypothetical navigation app.

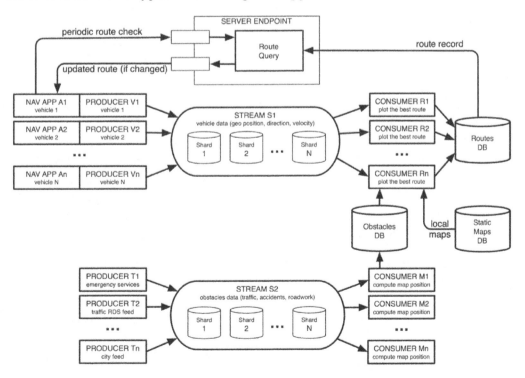

Here, the navigation app produces events containing vehicle's geo coordinates, as well as other data pertinent to its location (direction, velocity). In streaming architecture lingo, each app is a *Producer* of streaming data. Producers send individual *updates* (aka *events*) to a *stream* (aka *topic*). More than one stream could be created to organize the data by its type. In our example, all instances of the GPS navigation app send their data to the Stream S1 (vehicle data), while other producers (emergency services, traffic RDS, city feed) send their data to Stream S2 (obstacles data). To scale, each stream can be *sharded* (*partitioned*) into multiple *shards* (*partitions*). For simplicity, you can think of each shard as an independent server, and of a stream as a cluster of such servers. The more shards you have, the higher is the combined concurrent throughput of the stream. You can linearly scale the performance of your stream by increasing the number of shards. The data events received from producers are automatically distributed across shards and are persistently stored in the shards for subsequent processing.

The data events are then picked up by *consumers*. Think of consumers as processes or processing workers (threads) which *subscribe* to a particular stream; the stream feeds data to consumers, usually one event at a time, in near-FIFO order[24]. The more consumers you run, the more data events can be processed concurrently. The whole architecture scales linearly across consumers, just keep adding processing capacity. Some streaming frameworks allow consumers to receive more than one event at a time, which helps to avoid network congestion between the stream and the consumers.

In our example, there are two types of consumers – consumers of vehicle data (geo position, direction, velocity), and consumers of obstacles (traffic, accidents, and roadwork). Consumers of obstacles process the received data and populate a database of obstacles: which roads are closed, which are affected by heavy traffic or accidents, etc. This data is then used by the consumers of vehicle data to plot the best route. The routes are then stored in the database. The navigation app may periodically check for updates and receive the latest route available. Some systems may replace the periodic check by push message notifications.

Interestingly enough, different types of consumers can subscribe to the same event stream, for their own purposes. For instance, we may want to record a history of vehicle movements, to help find stolen vehicles. To implement this, our example

---

[24] FIFO ordering is only possible with a single shard. Multiple shards could be processed with varying speed, making strict FIFO impossible.

can be extended by adding consumers to the Stream S1 (vehicle data) to record the history or just the latest location. This opens up a larger opportunity to use event stream as a generic publish/subscribe mechanism. The system can publish various application events to a stream, and any number of subscribers can consume the events. For instance, publish an *order placed* event, and have (a) your fulfillment system process the order, (b) your marketing system send a confirmation email, and (c) the shipping system prepare the tracking label, all triggered concurrently. While it may be tempting to have a single stream serving as a unified messaging bus for the entire system, a better design is to dedicate independent streams for each event type. This way, your consumers receive only the event types they are subscribed to, giving you more fine-grained visibility of the workloads and more control over scaling.

Once you jump on the bandwagon of event streaming designs, you will find them quite useful, above and beyond the real-time applications. Some of the previously described design patterns, like logging solutions and processing of asynchronous portions of user-initiated transactions – are all good candidates to be implemented using event streaming.

Being a complex pattern, event streaming comes with its own quirks and complexities. Let's have a look at the most profound ones.

First, you must consider what happens if a consumer's code crashes. Typically, you have an option of writing it in two ways: you can make the streaming framework retry processing of an event, or you can allow the event to be lost. The former is preferred for business-critical data, the latter is commonplace for telemetry and IoT events which are continuously streamed and are harmless to lose. For instance, readouts of a temperature sensor usually can be lost without causing much harm, since the next readout is expected to follow shortly. Some streaming frameworks like Kinesis always retry but limit the number of retries. As we discussed in the earlier chapters, retries are safe if the consumer's code is idempotent. To make that work, you can use the design pattern described in Error Recovery (Chapter 8).

Second, you may inadvertently under-provision the number of consumers. With this, the events are ingested by the stream faster than they are consumed by consumers. This causes events pile up inside the stream, leading to increased latency. This is unacceptable for hard real-time systems but is generally ok for short time intervals in near-real-time implementations. If the increase in events is caused by a spike in traffic, then eventually the ingestion rate will go down, and the consumers will eventually catch up. You must have adequate means of monitoring your streams, telling you when its time to scale up – or having an autoscaling solution in place.

Some systems set a hard limit on how long an event can be persisted in a stream. For instance, Kinesis limits it to 48 hours. On the other hand, Kafka has no such hard limit, although you are still limited by the disk space available. Some architectures take advantage of this and use Kafka as the persistent Event Store, described in Datastore (Chapter 3).

Kinesis has its own very useful proprietary feature – it is fully integrated with Lambda Functions. With this integration, you need not manage or scale your consumers. The diagram below depicts how this works.

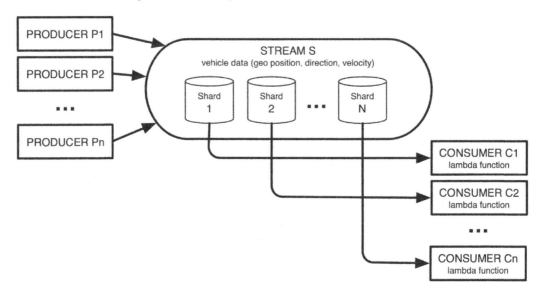

Essentially, every shard of the stream feeds a sequence of events to a single instance of your Lambda Function, acting as a consumer. If you have 10 shards, then you will have 10 Lambda instances to process the data. The beauty of this approach is that you need not scale your consumers independently of scaling the streams. Simply allocate enough shards to handle your maximum sustained load, and you are done. Another obvious benefit of this architecture is that it is entirely serverless, fully managed by Amazon Cloud.

We were talking a lot about scaling here, and streaming architectures scale linearly or near-linearly, assuming your consumers introduce no significant bottlenecks. However, to scale properly and on time, you must have sufficient telemetry built in, as well as an early warning system to alert you when your infrastructure requires additional capacity. Your architecture must have it all planned out. If you miss those critical pieces, your production operations could be compromised by insufficient capacity, or as another extreme you may burn too much cash on unnecessarily overprovisioned system.

<tldr>

There is almost always a place for event streaming as a part of your overall architecture, even if you are not building a real-time system. Streaming frameworks scale well through partitioning. Make stream processing logic idempotent to allow safe retries. Create means for monitoring and scaling of both streams and consumers.

https://anatoly.com/event-streaming

</tldr>

CHAPTER 11
CDN

> *Have you ever noticed that anybody driving slower than you is an*
> *idiot, and anyone going faster than you is a maniac?*
> – *George Carlin*

CDN stands for Content Delivery Network. It is a geographically distributed network of servers, used primarily for caching of static web assets. The most commonly cached web assets include images, video files, static HTML files, scripts, CSS files, and fonts.

Consider this diagram:

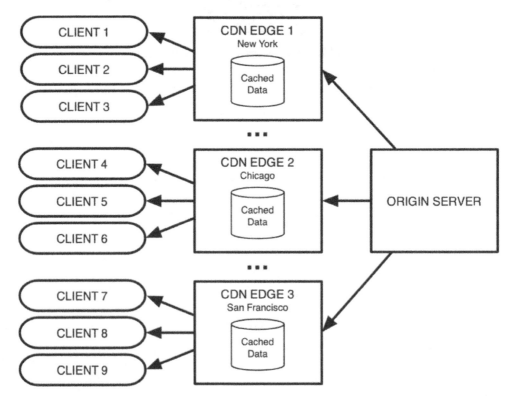

Here, the *origin server* is the server (or a farm of servers) running your application. CDN servers are distributed geographically, strategically placed in locations close to highly populated areas (large cities). Such locations are called *edges* of the CDN, and CDN servers located at edges are called *edge servers*. When you connect your origin server to a CDN, you are given a unique *dynamic CDN host name*. This host name is used in the client-side code for retrieving assets from your application. When a client connects to such dynamic CDN host name, the CDN's DNS server maps it into the IP address of the closest (in geographical sense) edge to the client. The edge server checks if it has the requested asset in its persistent cache. If it does, the asset is served back to the client directly from the edge location, without contacting the origin server. If the asset is not found in the edge's cache, then the request is forwarded to the origin server, which serves up the asset. When the response travels back, the asset may be cached by the edge server of the CDN, if you permit so. The later requests for the same asset from any client near the same edge are be served from the cache.

Good CDN networks have a large number of edge locations. For instance, AWS CloudFront has 176 edge locations worldwide, in 69 cities across 30 countries. In the real world, edge locations sometimes differ by their purpose: *network edges* vs *cache edges*. Network edge is a location where the CDN injects its traffic into the local Internet, whilst cache edge is a location where the actual persistent caching takes place.

Some CDNs like Fastly support two-tier caching approach, by introducing additional *shield* cache between edges and your system. This approach further reduces the number of requests that reach your system: as long as your system has served a static asset once, it will not have to do it again, until the cache expires. This helps to deploy large-scale solutions from a cold start when the traffic floodgates open and all the caches are still empty. This problem is frequently encountered when new software builds are deployed.

Shield caching is depicted in this diagram:

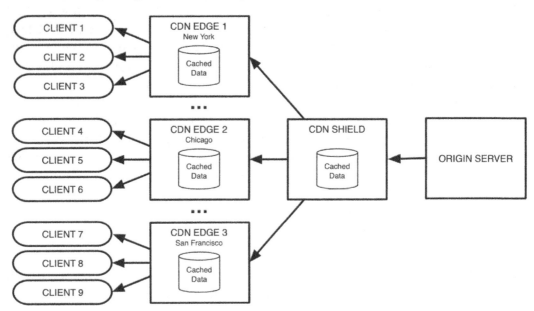

Caching is controlled by *caching headers* defined by HTTP protocol. Specifics of how they are configured are outside of this book's scope, but they are easy to find (google headers `cache-control`, `expires`, and `pragma`).

Another thing you need to know about all CDNs is that it is extremely expensive, inconvenient, and time-consuming to *invalidate the cached data* within CDN – and worse, it is impossible to remotely invalidate the cached data within the browser. Once a static asset is cached, it is not advisable to change it, and then attempt resetting the cache. It is much more productive to create a new asset (with a different name or retrieved with different URL parameters) and use it instead of the old one. There are two strategies I can recommend.

The first strategy applies to static assets like images and fonts. Those assets are typically files, hosted either on your servers or in a cloud storage location (such as AWS Simple Storage Service, aka S3). If you need to replace such asset, upload a new one, with a new name, and use that new name in your web pages and scripts. Then no cache reset will be required.

The second strategy applies to script bundles, CSS files, and other assets that change with every system build. For those, I recommend using a *cache buster* URL parameter. Imagine that your script bundle is included into your web page like this:

```
<script src="https://assets.mycompany.com/myScriptBundle.js?cb=1234" />
```

Here, the 1234 is either a build number, or a timestamp representing the build time, or just a random id generated at the beginning of your build process. The choice of the parameter name cb is arbitrary, you can call it build or anything else you like. Now, your bundle's file name remains the same, but CDN uses the entire URL as a cache key, and that key change when the cache buster value changes[25]. This way, your script bundle is cached until you rebuild the system next time. With the next build, the cache buster value will change, ensuring your pages receive a new version of the script bundle.

A slight variation of this technique is used when there is a need to support both the old and the new version of your script bundles, CSS, etc. This is useful when you deploy often, and you want the end user sessions which started with one version of the software to continue using it, without switching to the new release on the next page load. To support this, you can embed the cache buster into the name of your script bundle at build time, an allow for multiple versions of script bundles to co-exist. Here is how the script inclusion into your web page could look like:

```
<script src="https://assets.mycompany.com/myScriptBundle-1234.js" />
```

Some CDNs are more than just a distributed cache. For instance, CloudFront offers Lambda @Edge services, which allows you to run serverless code at edge locations, close to the end users. Another example is Fastly, which adds its own suit of features for manipulating both static and dynamic traffic. For certain specialized applications, such additional functionality might be essential, but the mainstream use of those features is to compensate for architectural deficiencies. If you get your architecture right, then you need none of those "fancy" features and services.

---

[25] In some CDNs like CloudFront, you have an option to control if the query parameters are included into or excluded from the cache key.

Always use CDN for delivery of static resources. Never reset the cache. Use cache busters to push changes through the CDN without a reset.

https://anatoly.com/cdn

CHAPTER 12
USER INTERFACES

Just 'cause you got the monkey off your back doesn't mean that the circus has left town.
– George Carlin

A few years back, I was building a service for wannabe celebrities. Each customer was getting their very own mobile app, for both iOS and Android, which allowed the fans to closely follow the lives of their favorite star in the form of video and photo posts. The app was also monetizable through advertising and in-app purchases of live video streams.

I focused my own efforts on the technology which generates mobile apps with a push of the button, and on the apps themselves. But I also needed to have a CMS – a content management system – for each celebrity to upload and manage their videos, photos, and stories. I had no capacity to do everything by myself, and I hired an offshore team of proven developers to build a web-based version of the CMS. We discussed all the specs and the integration points, and I gave the team the freedom to choose their tools. They picked Angular as the UI framework. The entire team was intimately familiar with Angular, and it was indeed the most popular UI framework at the time. On the server side of the CMS, the team chose Java and Spring, again very popular choices.

We launched the first version of the service rather quickly and had mild success with it. My business partner and I went to speak with the celebrities who were using the service and we identified several additional features to make our solution easier to market and monetize. The new features required several relatively minor enhancements to the CMS. My team rolled up the sleeves and went to work. They were supposed to deliver the changes in a month. Three months later, they were "almost there", and asked for another month. Another two months went by, and the team sent me a preview version that was terribly unstable and missing several important pieces of functionality. The updated CMS was incredibly unreliable, video uploads getting stuck from time to time, images disappearing without trace, and API calls from the mobile apps timing out half the time. It was a disaster.

I investigated. Turned out that the architecture involving Angular and Spring which my team put together was a terrible choice. Adding a field to a form or a button to the screen meant changing the code in 7 different places. Some of it was necessitated by Angular itself, and some by us using different programming languages on the client and server side, denying us any sharing of the interface definitions across platforms. If any of the changes were improperly made, there was no warning or error. The update either did not work at all, or it appeared functional, but then led to a data loss invisible to the user until they reengage with the system a few days later. I hated Angular, Spring, the whole world – but above all I despised myself for not working out the detailed architecture with the team.

My company had to bear the weight of serious setbacks and financial losses. We never rebuilt the CMS, and continued operating the earlier, more stable version of it. This line of business never took off, and we eventually switched to other opportunities.

<important>

User interfaces are by far the most frequent cause of excessive development and maintenance costs. Because of that, they require lots of undivided attention from the software architect.

</important>

Let's dive in.

The first question to ask yourself is the types of user interfaces you may need, now or in the future: *web* (browser-based), *mobile* (native apps for iOS, Android, etc.), *desktop* (native apps for Windows, OS X, Linux, etc.), *texting* (SMS, RMS, Facebook Messenger, Telegram, etc.), or *voice* (a good example is automated banking services provided via phone).

Web UI implementations require no installation, work everywhere, can be launched from a link embedded anywhere, and therefore represent the lowest-friction path for connecting with your customers. Web UI usually requires a live network connection, although there are ways how you can make it work offline (which I wouldn't recommend due to complexity and limited applicability).

Mobile apps have an edge of being installed on the customer's phone with full support for push messages and local reminders, having access to the mobile services and hardware, and being able to store data locally. Many of those features slowly become available in the browsers, stripping the benefits of the native apps over web UI, but at the time of this writing, there is still a huge gap. For instance, iOS 12 still does not support browser-based push messaging, and none of the browsers support local reminders.

Desktop apps these days become less and less popular. You may need one if you consume lots of resources, if you require the support of specialized hardware, if you must work with low-level features of the operating system, or if you interact directly with non-standard peripheral devices.

Texting apps including various chat bots, SMS texting, and instant messengers are on the rise. They are essentially a modern take on a very old computer interaction paradigm (a text terminal).

Voice Response Units (VRUs) represent a way to communicate via a voice line, making use of voice output and combined key and voice input from the end user.

For typical business solutions, you will need web-based UI and a mobile app. I will forego describing the options available for desktop, texting, and voice for the sake of simplicity.

Myriad options are available for building web-based UIs. Things become trickier when mobile apps are thrown into the mix. The two most popular platforms, iOS and Android, use entirely different programming languages, libraries, and tools. Building the apps independently for iOS and Android, plus separately a web UI, is wasteful and will require a lot of maintenance in the future. Here are the shortcuts that exist today:

Hybrid Mobile Apps: Code everything as a single-page web app. Use Apache Cordova[26] to run your web code on iOS and Android[27]. Use plugins available for Cordova to extend your web functionality into accessing native features of the phone which are not available in a browser. If no plugin is available for your purposes, develop your own one, by writing small snippets of native code for iOS and Android separately, but otherwise enjoy the common code base in JavaScript, HTML, and CSS. Use TypeScript to keep everything strongly typed. Use a reliable web development framework to build your UI; I recommend React/Redux. Mobile

---

[26] Another distribution of the same software is known as PhoneGap.

[27] Technically speaking, Cordova platform can support web and desktop targets, as well as several other mobile operating systems. However, most popular plugins are developed just for iOS and Android, which makes it a challenge to use Cordova beyond iOS and Android apps in practice.

apps which are constructed this way are called *Hybrid Apps*, as opposed to truly native ones. Hybrid apps are sometimes criticized for poor performance, although I built many hybrid apps which performed amazingly well. The key is not to abuse the mobile processor, keep everything clean and simple, and adopt the typical look & feel of a native app – which differs from the looks of a mobile web site.

React Native: Use React Native to build a native mobile app. It lets you to code across iOS and Android, and you have access to native plugins similar to those available in Cordova, or you can write your own. You can share your data types and some utility code across mobile and web but React Native is not the same as React Web, and therefore you end up having different UI implementations for the web and for the mobile apps. You can use TypeScript to keep everything strongly typed.

Flutter: Use Flutter for the mobile app development. Flutter produces native code for both iOS and Android, and it also supports native plugins – very similar to Cordova and React Native. Flutter's programming language is Dart, and your code base for the mobile apps will share nothing with your web UI. The interesting thing about Flutter is that it is backed by Google, and there are implementations underway to make Flutter work on the web and on the desktop. Those implementations have not reached maturity at the time of this writing, and I cannot recommend them as a proven path – but if you are reading this in 2020 or later, then there is a good chance that you could use Flutter for UI development across all platforms, web and mobile and desktop.

<important>

For most business solutions, Hybrid Mobile Apps is the most economical path. It allows you to reuse the code for the web and for the mobile platforms. For the remainder of this chapter, I will assume that you are moving forward with this option.

</important>

The next important thing to choose is the *UI framework*. In order to be compatible with mobile development, you should be building a single-page web app. This means the web page is loaded only once from the web server or from the mobile phone's local storage, and it is never refreshed or reloaded after that. All the UI changes play out within that single page.

The decision to build a single-page app helps narrowing down further choices of the UI frameworks. The good old jQuery is just too heavy for the job, and so is Angular and many others. The most lightweight and performing framework today, with broad range of third-party components available, is React/Redux. It gets a bit more complex and somewhat limiting where it comes to animations, especially transitional animations, but overall this provides you the fastest way forward. React is also great for code reuse, and Redux keeps your application state from sprouting through your entire codebase uncontrollably.

Getting a single-page app to *interact with your servers* in the most optimal way could be challenging when the code base is shared across web and mobile platforms. The sequence diagram below shows the right way of doing it.

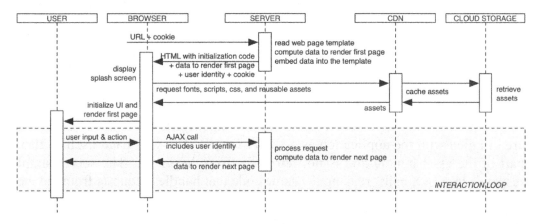

Here, the server receives an HTTP GET request from the browser, alongside with the cookies that carry user's identity from past interactions. The server returns a web page, usually built from a small template, by including the data necessary to render the first page into the web page itself. The server also returns a cookie which identifies the session and the end user, so that the next time the same user comes in, the server can customize the experience for that particular user. The web page, once received by the browser, immediately displays a splash screen, and loads scripts and other assets from a cloud storage or from your server, via CDN. Once all assets are loaded, the splash screen is replaced by a fully rendered first page. When a user interacts with the page, the collected input and actions are sent to the server via an AJAX call, alongside with the user identity, and the data received back is used to render the next page.

The described interaction pattern between the client and the server allows you to reuse the server-side code, and most of the client code, to work with a Cordova-based mobile app, as depicted in the next diagram.

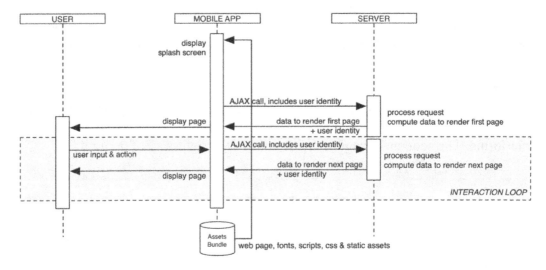

The main difference here is that assets are no longer retrieved online; instead they are installed with the application as an *asset bundle*. The web page itself is also a part of the asset bundle and is not retrieved from the server. The server simply responds to AJAX calls, reusing the same code that handles requests from the web app.

Another difference is in handling user identity. In web apps, the identity of the end user is most frequently stored in a cookie. Browser sends the cookie to the server alongside with the HTTP GET request for the web page, and the server may return a new or updated cookie alongside with its response. Cookies are automatically saved by the browser between requests and are retained for the duration of time you specify. In case of a mobile app, the page is stored locally, and the user identity must be passed to the server as a part of the AJAX call. To make the call reusable, pass user identity in the AJAX calls in both web and mobile versions, and process cookies server-side only on the initial page load in the web app.

The differences between the web and mobile UI code are also minor and can be contained in few methods of single pluggable interface.

Now, let's talk about the composition of the UI code. Wherever you look, the world is full of advice, which comes down to the Model-View-Controller (MVC) pattern, or one of its variations. It seems to be common wisdom that MVC is the answer to everything. MVC is also the pattern which my team used to build the CMS which I mentioned earlier – and failed. Let's have a look at it, on the high level, to make sure we are on the same page.

MVC suggests that your user interface code should comprise three components:

- **Model**: the data, or domain services that let you access the data (such domain services were referred to as Business Logic earlier in this book).

- **View**: the mechanism to display the data to the end user, and to accept input from the user.

- **Controller**: the algorithm which, on one hand, uses the input received from the user to manipulate the Model and, on another hand, provides data to the View.

This diagram illustrates how MVC is constructed:

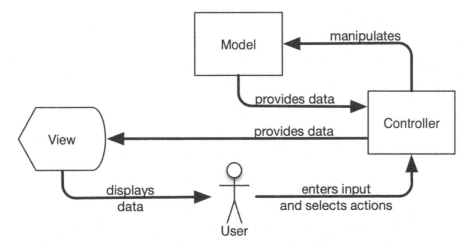

The main idea of MVC is a separation of concerns. It keeps all three components – the model, the view, and the controller – separate from each other. Here is how it does it.

The golden rule of MVC is: *The Model represents the data and does nothing else. The model does not depend on the view or on the controller.* This is an awesome guideline, totally in line with what we discussed earlier in the book (UI depends on Business Logic, not the other way around).

Where it comes to View, things get trickier. In theory, View should be independent of both Model and Controller and can be reusable. However, this rule is frequently violated by popular UI frameworks, and by developers who use those frameworks. It is also fairly common to merge the View and the Controller, which makes the View non-reusable. Long story short, a "clean" MVC implementation is a rare sight nowadays.

Besides the frequent misuse, MVC has several shortcomings of its own:

- MVC promises decoupling of components, while, in fact, Controller is tightly coupled with both View and Model (it depends on both).
- Controller in MVC violates the Single Responsibility Principle (remember the "S" in SOLID?) because it has two sources of change: Model (business logic) and View (user interface) and different people/teams behind them (product vs UI/UX).
- MVC causes Controller code grow uncontrollably (pun intended). This is known as *Massive View Controller* problem.
- MVC does not promote reusability.
- MVC significantly reduces the testability of the code.

Because of these shortcomings, we've seen lately a proliferation of MVC-derived patterns that somewhat improve the original, such as MVP, MVVM, MVI, and numerous others. Confusing, isn't it?

<important>

Forget the MVC-derived acronyms. There is a better way[28].

</important>

Imagine that you are asked to engineer a process for interacting with an end user via snail mail. You came up with a set of forms, which are mailed to the end user, one at a time. When the user receives a form, they fill it out, and send it back. When you receive the filled-out form back from the user, you first check the form for

---

[28] Maybe someone already came up with an acronym for the pattern described further in this chapter. If you know one, please drop me a line.

errors. If there are errors in the form, you highlight the errors, and re-send the same form to the user again, asking them to make corrections. If the form is error-free, then you record its content somewhere, and decide which should be the next form to send. Some forms could be rudimentary and require no user input – such as a thank you letter, a promise to get back to them in 30 days, etc.

What if we map this very logical physical process to the technology world? Let's give it a shot.

- First, we must implement the digital representation of a form – let's call them *form views*. Form views are implemented in the client. Since we are building a single-page app (web or mobile), we must implement all the form views within that single-page app. Our web page will have to contain all the code necessary to display every form view we intend to display in our app. Forms views could be reusable. For instance, we can have one universal form for collecting multiple choice answers from the user, and we can use this form in a variety of contexts.

- Then, we have our *business logic*. The business logic is implemented in the server; it interacts with the *data model* internally, as we discussed in the earlier chapters. The data model is not directly consumable by the UI.

- Now we must come up with a way to exchange the data between the business logic and form views. For that, we create *form adapters*. Each form adapter has two functions: (1) to prefill and customize the forms before they are displayed to the end user, and (2) when the user takes action, to read the form data, validate it, and either reject the form with an error or call the business logic to process. Note that while forms views are reusable, form adapters are not – they are custom-written for each interaction with the user. Form adapters serve as bindings between reusable form views and the business logic of your application.

- Finally, we need a single *router* to decide which form adapter (and therefore which form) should be used at any given time. The router must communicate with the business logic to support its decisions. For instance, during a new user registration process, the router may sequentially ask the user to enter their name, email, and password.

The topology of this solution is depicted in the diagram below.

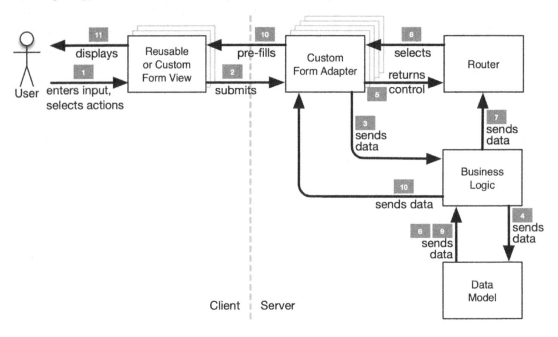

To illustrate how this pattern functions, consider this diagram:

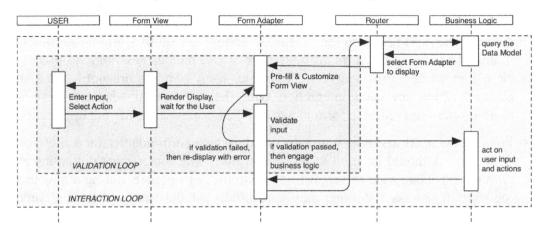

This model works very well with React – simply use React/Redux to build your Form Views as React components. Each Form View, in turn, can be assembled from third-party or proprietary lower-level components.

This design pattern does not rely on React in any way; you can use a UI framework of your choice, as long as you limit its use to building Form Views.

Finally, let's consider dependencies between modules, as depicted below:

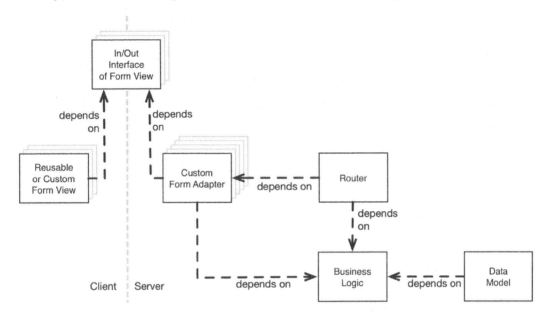

As you can see, we have solved or reduced most of the problems exhibited by MVC, while retaining all the benefits it promised and more:

- All components are properly decoupled; both the Form View (View in MVC) and the Business Logic (Model in MVC) remain decoupled from everything else.

- The Business Logic remains the core dependency of other components (the Model in MVC depends on nothing).

- Views are standardized and made reusable, while retaining the possibility of creating custom ones if necessary.

- The monolithic Controller from MVC is broken down into multiple Custom Form Adapters and a single Router, preventing the Massive View Controller problem.

- Navigation decisions are now contained in the Router and are cleanly segregated from data input and display.

- The Router still violates the Single Responsibility Principle, just like the Controller in MVC, but the Router is a much smaller component, keeping the blast radius from such violation relatively small.

- The Custom Form Adapter's dependency on the interface of Form View is not expected to be a source of significant change, due to the fixed nature of the Form View's contract. While technically it could be viewed as violating the Single Responsibility Principle, in practice its primary reason to change is the Business Logic. Additionally, since each of the Custom Form Adapters depend on a single Form View's interface only, the blast radius from a change in an interface is small.

<breakpoint/>

Now, let's discuss how to control the *look & feel* of your UI. The first knee-jerk reaction is to continue on the traditional path of shared CSS. It's easy – you change your CSS, and everything changes automatically, right? Wrong.

Generally speaking, shared CSS is a terrible idea for large software systems. Here is why:

- CSS only works in HTML-based implementations. It works with Cordova which shares the code with the web, but it doesn't work with Flutter or with any of the native mobile components. If you plan to build true native apps, you need an alternative mechanism. With Cordova, you may also find that some components are implemented natively via native plugins and do not respond to CSS changes.

- The CSS which is written for a component, and the HTML generated by the same component are tightly coupled but their coupling is not validated in any reliable way. When a component's implementation changes, your CSS markup may cease to function, without notice.

- In rich interfaces, each UI component should be skinnable. For instance, a button component must be of different colors depending on which background it is placed on. To achieve this in CSS, the most commonplace approach is to use CSS selectors which reference HTML structure (selectors like *X child of Y parent*). Such selectors tend to break every time the nesting of UI components change, or the components themselves change. Finally, CSS selectors are tied to the underlying HTML implementation, breaking the encapsulation of design decisions made by component designers. Upgrade to a new version of a third-party component can have devastating effects on your UI.

- There are cases when you may want to share certain styling properties across components, but individually control others. For instance, form's background, font of form labels, and default text color are usually controlled uniformly across all components on the form, while other styles remain component specific. It is incredibly hard to get all components consistently designed to depend on the same CSS properties to enable sharing.

A better way is to make your UI components directly skinnable. Think of your components accepting a parameter (a property in React) that represents a *skin*, i.e., a collection of parameters, usually in JSON format, which completely controls your component's look and feel. Skinning of HTML components could be done via inline CSS styling, eliminating the need for a separate style sheet. Skinning of native mobile components is usually done by setting native properties of those components. Flutter has its own styling mechanisms represented by several library classes – which can easily integrate with your proprietary skin.

You can also break skinning data into two sections – *Individual Skin* vs *Ambient Skin*. Individual Skin is responsible for properties specific to each individual component, while Ambient Skin contains shared styling for a larger area of the screen, such as a form, or a row in a list or a table.

Since skins are just data, they can be computed. You can devise an algorithm to compute some of the skin values. This is useful if you want to adjust font sizes based on the size of the screen or to support accessibility settings.

A word of warning: do not confuse skin and layout. Skin should contain no information which controls positioning of UI components. Layouts should always be implemented in the logic of the UI components, or they can rely on proven HTML layouts, or layout libraries in native apps. Skin may affect the layout, for instance by altering a font size, but it should not be used to control the layout.

Finally, a note on responsive designs. Responsive designs are great, but they are insufficient in many cases. Entire end-user workflows may require a different approach for desktop vs mobile. For instance, you may display a long registration form at once to a desktop user, but prompt the user the enter one field at a time on mobile platform. In some cases, you may want to support tablets as a separate category as well. The differentiators between devices is not only the screen size, but also touch vs pointer capability, and on-screen keyboard vs physical keypad. Touch interfaces invalidate some of the traditional way of displaying information such as tooltips and alternating colors on pointer flyovers. On-screen keyboards require you to reserve enough space on the screen for the keyboard to open, since it may overlay a large portion of the screen. This is why many mobile apps show forms one fields at a time. Keyboards also generally prevent you from creating designs with action buttons placed at the bottom of the screen, while it is very typical for desktop-optimized UI.

Optimizing user experience through altering user workflows beyond just the screen layout does not come for free. In the UI architecture pattern described here, you have two options. One, you can build create different routers for different device types (mobile, desktop, perhaps tablet). Two, you can create smarter form views, which have built-in device optimizations, but appear to the rest of the system as a single view. For instance, the router tells the UI to display the registration form view, but the view itself is smart enough to create a step-by-step experience on a mobile device, but a single-step long form on desktop.

<tldr>

User Interface must be properly architected, and under no circumstances can be left to sprout organically without governance. You can maximize code reuse across web and mobile apps by using Apache Cordova. There is a better UI code composition pattern than MVC. Consider programmable skinning instead of shared CSS. Mobile vs desktop differences go beyond screen sizes, and may require different user flows.

https://anatoly.com/user-interfaces

</tldr>

CHAPTER 13
MICROSERVICES

> *Death is caused by swallowing small amounts of saliva over a long*
> *period of time.*
> *— George Carlin*

You have definitely heard of microservices, or maybe had a chance of working on a microservices-based architectures. Essentially, microservices are based on the old idea of service-oriented architecture (SOA) taken to the extreme. The idea is to replace software modules with API endpoints. So instead of importing a module and using its functionality directly, you are calling an API, usually via HTTP protocol. The promises of microservices are:

- Use containerization to easily deploy services (which is the benefit of containerization, not of microservices themselves).

- Services can be coded in different languages, they are technology and infrastructure agnostic (which is absolutely true; this is almost the only reliable way to mix different programming languages in a single server-side environment[29]).

- Each service can be scaled independently (true, with a caveat: scaling a "flat" microservices infrastructure is easy; scaling daisy-chained microservices could be extremely challenging).

- Services can be developed independently from one another (true, although this can be achieved without the complexity of microservices: independent development of components can be facilitated through a basic discipline in applying SOLID principles).

On top of somewhat arguable benefits, microservices bring their own spectrum of problems:

---

[29] There exist experimental alternatives, like GraalVM, which allows you to execute and interoperate multiple languages within the same virtual machine.

- API calls over the network are slow and may lead to network congestion.
- Managing dependencies could be hard; there is no compile-time detection of incompatibilities.
- Much harder to test and monitor than traditional architectures.
- Nearly impossible to carry transactions across API calls[30].
- Insufficient scaling of one service leads to scalability problems and frequently to a failure of other services which depend on it. This is known as *backpressure*.

There is a lot of confusion in the field around microservices, leading to many misguided decisions. Specifically, infrastructure is confused with code segregation. Code segregation does not have to be affecting the infrastructure. There are other – simpler – ways to achieve it, including those covered in this book. In the past, it made sense to run service code close to the physical location of the data, which used to be the same server – hence microservices as a way to build *infrastructure*. This design pattern is rarely applicable nowadays, since most databases are now hosted separately from the application code. BTW, you can view the database as a microservice of its own, which your code depends on.

In my opinion, microservices (or just API services) fit well for the following purposes:

- Servicing the client tier (i.e. implementation of the API servicing the UI implementation)
- Exposing APIs to third parties
- Representing third-party services
- Representing services built in a technology stack incompatible with the core stack used by your system
- Representing legacy systems and components

I wouldn't, however, venture into artificially breaking up an otherwise well-designed architecture into microservices – unless you know exactly what you are doing and why.

---

[30] Transactions are typically tracked by database engines on per-connection basis, and each microservice typically requires its own connection. It is possible to create a database proxy service which handles transactions across microservices, but this approach comes with significant performance, scalability, and reliability risks.

Microservices are infrastructure and deployment strategy, not an architecture pattern. They are great for building APIs and integrations.

</important>

If, however, you end up with microservices, you must at least ensure that you detect API incompatibilities at compile time. If you are using the same language across the board, and the language supports interfaces, then you should simply separate the interface definitions from service implementation and import those definitions by services and consumers alike.

If you are dealing with services and consumers written in different languages, then you need a single source of truth for your API data structures. The most typical approach is to use an *Interface Definition Language (IDL)*. There are not so many good IDLs out there. One of the popular ones is *Protocol Buffers* (aka *Protobufs*). You can define your APIs using Protobufs, and then generate interfaces and bindings for almost any popular language. Another approach is to use one of the strongly typed languages which supports *reflection*[31] (like Java or C#) to define your API, and then use reflection mechanisms of the language to generate compatible data structures for other languages. This effectively turns your Java or C# code into an IDL.

<tldr>

Microservices could be dangerous, and their benefits are arguable. If you are inexperienced with microservices, stay away. If you do microservices across multiple programming languages, use IDL to keep all APIs in sync.

https://anatoly.com/microservices

</tldr>

---

[31] Reflection means inspection of classes, interfaces, fields and methods at runtime without knowing the names of those classes, interfaces, fields, methods at compile time.

CHAPTER 14
API

Careful, if you think too much, they'll take you away.
– George Carlin

Every time I think of APIs (Application Programming Interfaces), I mentally go back to 2009-2010 when I was working on my social media marketing platform. A fair amount of functionality of the platform was tied to Facebook, and it made extensive use of Facebook API to do its magic. From my experience, I always thought of vendor APIs as something sacred (in this context well-designed, well-tested, backward compatible, and reliable). Facebook shattered that shiny mental construct which I carried in my head for many years. Their API changed frequently, with little advance warning. The changes were breaking and weren't backward compatible. I was pulling my hair out with each update, and we had to rewrite a lot of code to keep my high-profile clients happy. At the time, I was working with Mountain Dew, Gatorade, FOX, and Millennium Entertainment, amongst others – and having a system downtime was simply not an option.

Over time, Facebook became better in planning their API upgrades, but the changes were still breaking. Worse, significant chunks of functionality were removed with almost every new version published. In all fairness, this was a logical reflection of the company's growth, as they were discovering their true place under the sun, the value of the data they have, and monetization methods they wanted to keep exclusively to themselves. The technical execution, however, could have been much smoother.

This experience taught me to pay serious attention to stability and backward compatibility of the APIs, at least those exposed for third-party consumption.

Every API is a contract. In that, it is similar to an interface in your programming language, with one important distinction: changes to an API may break not only technical contracts but legal contracts as well. Changes of an API must always be coordinated with the consuming party, or – better – you shall be backward-compatible in your changes.

</important>

For this book, I define the term API as a *contract exposed by one software component for the purposes of consumption by another software component.* In a general sense, it can be anything – a software library, a documentation for making network calls to a server, or almost anything else. Here, we will focus squarely on the APIs exposed as HTTP endpoints on the network.

You have probably heard about REST, which stands for **R**epresentational **S**tate **T**ransfer. REST leverages HTTP protocol by treating services as resources with CRUD operations (Create, Read, Update, Delete) available on them, expressed as HTTP PUT, GET, POST and DELETE methods respectively. For instance, you can build an API which creates new users by sending a POST method, updates by sending a PUT, reads by using GET, and deletes with DELETE. As you may recall from previous chapters, a CRUD data model is not always the best approach, which makes REST frequently a poor choice as well. The benefit of REST is that, by closely following HTTP guidelines, it is compatible with CDN caching. You can leverage this aspect of REST for idempotent data retrieval and search functions, implemented using HTTP GET method, if there is need. Other than that, you get very little benefit from building your API around the REST pattern.

I recommend a different approach to API construction, which is not REST-compliant. In exchange, it allows you to overcome many shortcomings of the traditional REST approach. If you ever need CDN caching for your API responses, then you can create another flavor of your API, a subset, which includes only GET methods, and which is fully compliant with REST[32].

In this chapter, we will look at how to construct a good service API. We are not going to concern ourselves with the transport layer and marshalling/unmarshalling of the data. Instead, we will focus on API data structures. In the interest of

---

[32] APIs which are fully compliant with REST are frequently called RESTful.

simplicity, we assume that the data is transferred in JSON format using HTTP POST.

While constructing a good API, we must consider:

- Unified approach to all API calls
- Error handling
- Stability and backward compatibility
- Ability to submit multiple calls in a single request
- Ability to ship client-side logs to the server alongside with any request
- Ability to ship server-side logs to the client alongside with any response
- Ability to programmatically analyze error responses
- Ability to create new API versions instead of making breaking changes
- Security

Let's start with error handling. If you want your client code to have visibility into the cause of server-side errors, forget about using HTTP codes as responses. Those codes shall be reserved for infrastructure failures. From the infrastructure point of view, any attempt to withdraw an amount that exceeds the account balance is not an error – it's a success and should return HTTP 200 OK. Application-specific errors must be handled through the data returned in the API response.

Now, let's build a sample API which performs Read and Update operations on a user profile. First, we create a module `api-defs` which defines all API data structures. There is a reason we want to place all API definitions in a separate module: the *API data structures should have no dependencies*, period. Your API definitions module must have no imports. You should never ever the use data structures from any layer of your system or from any third party library for API definitions. Doing so puts the API contract at risk of unexpected changes when those dependencies change, breaking the contract with third parties who consume your API.

In our example, the module containing all API definitions may look like this:

```
<code>
// module api-defs.ts

interface LogData {
  entries: string[];
}
```

```
export enum QueryType {
  READ_PROFILE, UPDATE_PROFILE
};
interface Query {
  qt : QueryType;
};
export interface ReadProfileQuery extends Query {
  qt : QueryType.READ_PROFILE;
  profileId : string;
};
export interface UpdateProfileQuery extends Query {
  qt : QueryType.UPDATE_PROFILE;
  profileId : string; // id of the profile to update
  userName? : string; // new name, omit to retain previous value
  userAge? : number; // new age, omit to retain previous value
};
export enum ResultType {
  PROFILE
};
export enum ProfileQueryOutcome {
  SUCCESS, NOT_FOUND
};
interface Result {
  rt : ResultType;
};
export interface Profile {
  userName : string | null;
  userAge : number | null;
};
export interface ProfileResult extends Result {
  rt : ResultType.PROFILE;
  outcome : ProfileQueryOutcome;
  profile : Profile | null; // null allowed on failure
};
export interface Request {
  requestId : string; // unique ID (usually UID), pass the same value on retry
  logData : LogData | null; // ships client-side log to the server
  queries : {
    [queryId : string] : ReadProfileQuery | UpdateProfileQuery;
  };
};
export interface Response {
  requestId : string; // echos the ID passed in the request, for validation
```

```
    logData : LogData | null; // ships server-side log to the client
    results : {
      [queryId : string] : ProfileResult;
    }
};
```
</code>

This module contains all the data structures for the API and is intended to be imported by both client-side and server-side code, to keep them in sync. If the client-side code is written in a different language, then the matching data structures would have to be defined again in that language, or both definitions could be generated from a single source in an IDL (for example, in Protobufs).

The data structures which are transmitted between the client and the server are Request and Response, respectively.

Each Request may trigger the execution of several business functions at once. For that purpose, we created the Query interface, which is an abstraction for any business function. Multiple queries can be submitted by the client in the same instance of the Request object. To make it easy for the client to match the returned results to each submitted query, we identify queries by queryId, which the client can set arbitrarily, and the server must echo back with each query result.

In our example, we implement two business functions – reading and updating a user profile – which are represented by ReadProfileQuery and UpdateProfileQuery, respectively. The UpdateProfileQuery does not require all profile fields to be present; it only updates those set by the client. To determine which query is received on the server side, we use the enumerated value QueryType, included with each query.

Now, let's illustrate the use of this API on the client side. In the interest of simplicity, we send a request with a single read query, to retrieve the user profile with profileId==12345. We will be using a library that implements httpCall() function to submit a request to the server, and to receive the response. Here is the code:

<code>
```
import { ProfileQueryOutcome, ProfileResult,
         QueryType, ReadProfileQuery,
         Request, Response, ResultType } from './api-defs';
import { httpCall } from './http';
import { getLogStrings, printLogStrings } from './logger';
import { getUid } from './uid';
```

```
let rq : Request = {
  requestId : getUid(),
  logData : { entries : getLogStrings() },
  queries : {
    'read' : <ReadProfileQuery>{
      qt : QueryType.READ_PROFILE,
      profileId : `12345`
    }
  }
};

let rs : Response =
  httpCall( `api.mycompany.com/profile`, rq ) as Response;

if( rs.logData ) {
  printLogStrings( rs.logData.entries );
}

let result = rs.results[ 'read' ];

switch( result.rt ) {
  case ResultType.PROFILE:
    let readProfileResult = result as ProfileResult;
    switch( readProfileResult.outcome ) {
      case ProfileQueryOutcome.SUCCESS: {
        console.log( `name: ${ readProfileResult.profile.userName }` );
        console.log( `age: ${ readProfileResult.profile.userAge }` );
        break;
      }
      case ProfileQueryOutcome.NOT_FOUND: {
        console.log( `user profile not found` );
        break;
      }
    }
    break;
  default:
    throw new Error( `unexpected result type ${ result.rt }` );
}
```
</code>

Notice the use of ResultType. The way we constructed the API, the same function could return different data types in response. In our case, the returned data type is always the same (ResultType.PROFILE) and we could eliminate the outer switch statement. I however decided to keep it as a sanity check, and to demonstrate where varying result types should be handled.

Also notice that the server-side log is shipped to the client, and is printed immediately after receiving the response from the server. As it was explained earlier, this gives us a chance to troubleshoot server-side problems at development time without digging through server-side logs.

Finally, let's consider the server-side code:

```
<code>
import { ProfileQueryOutcome, ProfileResult,
         QueryType, ReadProfileQuery,
         Request, Response, ResultType,
      UpdateProfileQuery } from './api-defs';
import { getLogStrings, printLogStrings } from './logger';
import { readUser, updateUser, User } from './user-model-defs';

export const handleRequest = ( rq : Request ) : Response => {
  // skipping handling of rq.requestId in the interest of simplicity
  if( rq.logData ) {
    printLogStrings( rq.logData.entries );
  }
  let rs : Response = {
    requestId : rq.requestId,
    logData : null,
    results : {}
  };
  for( let queryId in rq.queries ) {
    let query = rq.queries[ queryId ];
    let user : User = null;
    switch( query.qt ) {
      case QueryType.READ_PROFILE: {
        let readProfileQuery = query as ReadProfileQuery;
        user = readUser( readProfileQuery.profileId );
        break;
      }
      case QueryType.UPDATE_PROFILE: {
        let updateProfileQuery = query as UpdateProfileQuery;
        user = readUser( updateProfileQuery.profileId );
        if( updateProfileQuery.userName != undefined ) {
          user.name = updateProfileQuery.userName;
        }
        if( updateProfileQuery.userAge != undefined ) {
          user.age = updateProfileQuery.userAge;
        }
        updateUser( user );
        break;
      }
    }
    let result : ProfileResult;
    if( user ) {
      result = {
        outcome : ProfileQueryOutcome.SUCCESS,
```

```
          rt : ResultType.PROFILE,
          profile : {
            userName : user.name,
            userAge : user.age
          }
        };
      }
      else {
        result = {
          outcome : ProfileQueryOutcome.NOT_FOUND,
          rt : null,
          profile : null
        };
      }
      rs.results[ queryId ] = result;
    }
    rs.logData = { entries : getLogStrings() };
    return rs;
  };
</code>
```

Here, we implemented a server-side request handler `handleRequest()`. It prints the client-side log, and then processes all received queries in a loop. Different types of queries are processed independently by query type, using the `switch` statement. The request handler returns a response containing the results of all queries, each identifiable by the `queryId` originally received from the client. Server response includes a copy of server-side log.

This example only illustrates the approach. It lacks some important pieces, such as server-side code that will make the service idempotent in case of retries, and client-side code to retry the call in a case of an error. Client-side code also lacks network error handling. You may also consider executing multiple queries concurrently (asynchronously) in the server-side logic, as long as the queries have no mutual interdependencies. This can significantly reduce server-side latency of your API calls with multiple queries.

I am leaving it up to you to think through those additional pieces.

If you plan to expose your API to third parties, then you must consider backward compatibility of the *future versions*. The easiest way to ensure backward compatibility is to create new API request & response interfaces for each new version and support all versions simultaneously on the server side. This way, you can handle the traffic carrying any version of the API ever existed. You can then officially deprecate older versions, give your API consumers plenty of time to migrate to the new API, and eventually make the old versions respond with an error and stop supporting them.

If your API is expected to be consumed massively, it makes sense to provide third-party developers with additional tooling. The most useful tool you can give them is a language-specific binding (or several, for multiple languages), in a form of a pre-packaged library. Such libraries are frequently called *SDKs* (*Software Development Kits*). For instance, you can publish your SDKs for Java, JavaScript/TypeScript, Python, C/C++, and whatever other languages you expect to be useful to your customers. Every time you create a new version of your API, you release a new version of the SDK for each of the supported languages. Ideally, your SDK should be backward-compatible the same way as your API is. The SDK shall not be required to work with your API; you must always allow third-party developers to connect with your API directly, thus eliminating the need for you to support all possible programming languages under the sun.

Another important consideration when building an API is *security*. Security concerns include *encryption*, *authentication*, *authorization*, and *rate limiting*.

Encryption makes sure the API messages cannot be deciphered if intercepted by a third party, as a part of a *man-in-the-middle attack*. This makes the API safe to use over the public Internet. The most common API encryption solution today is TLS (aka SSL) protocol, which encrypts all communications between a client and a server. You can tell if TLS is used by looking at the HTTP URL of an API endpoint. If the client can only connect using `https:` protocol (i.e., the URL begins with `https://...`) then the connection is encrypted with TLS. If the client can connect to the API using `http:` protocol, then it is not secure. Note that the secure part of your API message is the body, but not the URL itself – thus one should never include any sensitive information such as passwords or security tokens directly into the URLs.

Authentication safeguards your API against use by unauthenticated clients, protecting the API from abuse by the parties who has no right to access it. The most simplistic form of authentication is the *Basic Authentication* in HTTP. Basic

Authentication passes HTTP Authorization header which consists of the word Basic followed by a space and a base64-encoded string which contains user name, colon, and password (i.e., username:password). For instance:

```
< output >
Authorization: Basic aND1lcwsdarFDSERsdf89a==
</output>
```

Basic Authentication is commonplace, but it has a significant flaw: the username and password have to be stored by the client, and you have no say over how they do it. I've seen a lot of code with hard-coded username and password values, which was posted in a publicly accessible Github repository – making the API wide open for malicious exploits.

As a commonplace alternative to Basic Authentication which many APIs rely on is *API Keys*. API Keys are randomly generated values, which are passed from the client to the server as a part of an encrypted request. The API keys are then processed on the application level, which gives you a chance to use them not only for authentication but also for authorization purposes (as explained below). While this approach is widely accepted, it suffers from the same risk of the client mishandling them.

A more secure approach available for server-to-server communications is *client certificates*. This is an extension of the TLS protocol. You may have noticed that when you connect to a secure site from your browser using secure URLs, the browser usually displays a padlock icon indicating the connection is secure. Clicking on the icon allows you to view the *server certificate*, which ensures you are indeed connected with the desired server, and not with a malicious impersonator. A similar mechanism exists for the server to validate the legitimacy of the client, by the client exposing its *client certificate*. Your server then validates the client-side certificate as a part of the TLS handshake, and a connection cannot be established if the certificate is invalid or missing. This approach is secure but could be hard to execute in certain infrastructures, especially in serverless ones.

An even tighter security can be achieved by *IP Address Whitelisting*, although it becomes less and less popular with the proliferation of dynamic server provisioning in the cloud. This approach configures a list of allowed client IP addresses, or ranges of IP addresses, in the firewall, or on the server. Then the inbound connections are only allowed from the whitelisted IP addresses. This approach has seen a lot of popularity in the past, but has become much harder to implement recently, since it requires the clients to fall into a stable well-known range of IP addresses. It is hard to impose such requirement onto third parties which consume your API.

For the APIs called from the client tier (such as browser or mobile apps), the most popular way to authenticate is by using *token-based credentials*. Here is the diagram illustrating this process:

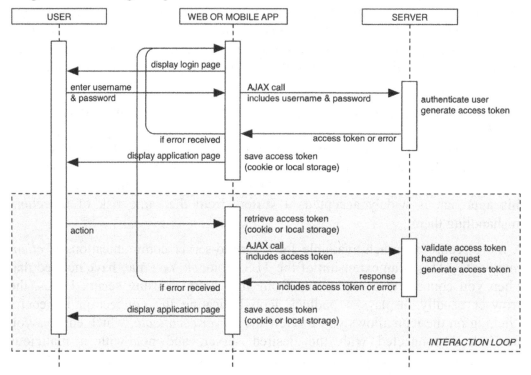

Here is how it works. First, the user gets authenticated by either logging in using their username and password, or via a password-less system where the user receives a code via an SMS message or in an email, which they must re-enter into the login screen. In response to a successful login, the client is given a *token*, usually a character string produced by the server. Tokens are usually generated by encrypting a data structure containing the user identity, their access rights, and the access expiration time. The client then passes the token to all subsequent API calls. When the server receives the token, it decrypts it. If decryption fails, then the token is invalid, the server responds with authentication error, and the client forces the user to re-login. If decryption succeeds, then the server checks the expiration time of the token and refuses to service the request if the token has expired; the client receives an error and forces the user to re-login. Otherwise, the server handles the request. When finished, the server generates a new encrypted token with the new expiration time and returns it back to the client as a part of the response. The client then uses the new token for the next API call. The client can store the token in a cookie or in the local storage, to keep the user logged in even if they close their browser window and re-open it later. With this approach, the user retains access to the API as long as they are actively using the system, with no limitation. If, however, the user is inactive for an period of time which exceeds the token's expiration, then the server refuses to service the request, and the client forces the user to re-login.

Finally, on the topic of authentication: there are also *OAuth1 and OAuth2 protocols*. They aren't two versions of the same, but two distinctively different protocols, OAuth1 is more secure but is also more complex to implement than OAuth2. These protocols are primarily intended for *platforms*, where access rights are granted by the system which the end user already has access to, to another system which acts on the user's behalf. You may have encountered OAuth2 more than once already, by giving access to your Google Drive to third party applications. OAuth protocols issue an *access token* similar to an API Key, but since the token is issued dynamically at runtime, the risk of it ending up hard-coded and exposed through source code is low. Implementing an OAuth protocol is far more involving than a simple API Key, but you absolutely should consider it if you are building a platform with extensive API use by third parties.

Authorization provides more granular control over which services and data are available to a specific API client (or user). Authorization is usually implemented in the business logic. Each client (or user) is assigned a list of business functions or data entities which they have access to. Such lists are also known as *access control lists* or *ACLs*. When dealing with human end users, ACLs are frequently assigned indirectly, through the use of *user roles*. The idea behind user roles is to identify typical access rights for various roles the users have in the system (basic users, administrators, accounting, superusers, etc.), specify ACLs once for each role, and assign roles to the individual users. This simplifies maintenance. Imagine that you added several new features to your system. When ACLs are managed individually for each user, you will have to adjust those ACLs for each user to give them access. Alternatively, you only need to adjust ACLs for a few roles, even if there are thousands or millions of users with that role.

In many cases, you may want to hide inaccessible features and data from the end users in the UI. Regardless, you shall process all security considerations on the server side. ACLs should never be exposed to the client-side code. Instead, your business logic on the server shall provide clear instructions for showing/hiding specific UI elements. The protected data shall never reach the client. Client-side code is relatively open for hacking, and your architecture should not be exposed to a security breach in case client-side validations are overridden by a hacker.

Rate limiting is a way of capping the number of API calls which a client can make in a given period of time. Sometimes it is done to support multiple pricing tiers, but more frequently to protect the API from abuse and from denial of service attacks (DOS). Rate limiting is best controlled outside of the application layer, through firewall hardware or using cloud safeguards. You can implement different strategies for rate limiting, from connection rejections to automatic throttling.

To wrap up the API topic, a brief note on **GraphQL**. For those unfamiliar, GraphQL was originally developed by Facebook in 2012, and then open-sourced in 2015. It creates a way to build an API as a structured data query, while the server-side implementation (typically in Node.js) does the leg work of interpreting those queries. GraphQL is frequently used for aggregation of legacy and third-party APIs, and it creates a seemingly easy path to host multiple API functions on a single HTTP endpoint. So – what about GraphQL? Frankly, I am not a fan. GraphQL inverts the dependency chain, making the development of a server-side business logic driven by the needs of a client. This contradicts many core architecture principles described in this book. If you buy into those principles, then there should be no place for GraphQL in your blueprints. Besides, GraphQL is hard to scale, it doesn't have a strong type binding to your programming language (i.e., the errors will not be caught at compile time) and it is incompatible with CDN caching mechanisms. The flexibility of getting a subset of data can be easily modeled using the straightforward API approach which I described earlier in this chapter, without breaking any of the core architecture principles. The approach suggested in this book also works on a single endpoint, just like GraphQL does.

`<tldr>`

REST is rarely required in real world. Follow the pattern of API construction explained by example in this chapter. Consider providing your API's customers an SDK. Keep your API secure. Try to resist GraphQL's charms.

https://anatoly.com/api

`</tldr>`

CHAPTER 15
BATCH

If someone with multiple personalities threatens to kill himself, is it considered a hostage situation?
– George Carlin

Have you heard the term *batch processing*? If not, you might have heard of *cron jobs* or *daemon processes*, which are not exactly the same thing, but close.

<important>

Batch processing is a pattern of processing transactions in a group (a "batch"). No user interaction takes place once batch processing is underway. This differentiates batch processing from online transaction processing, which handles transactions one at a time, and allows for user input for each individual transaction.

</important>

In the early 1990s, I was a software developer on the team tasked with building a banking system. Traditionally in banking, lots of data processing is done in batch. Batch usually runs at night and processes massive amounts of transactions. Easy, right? Well, in our case, batch processing was a ticking bomb, we just didn't know it at the time.

The client's requirement was to fit all batch processing into a 4-hour batch window, from midnight to 4 am Pacific; they wanted everything finished by 7 am Eastern Time, one hour before the opening time on the East Coast. We did better. We could complete all the batch processing for 2x the projected number of transactions within 3 hours.

All went well; we launched the system, and it worked amazingly well for the first 6 months. Then our customer merged with another bank, three times larger in operation, and the merged entity decided to run our beautiful new shiny banking system across all branches of the merged business. This would quadruple our licensing fees – awesome news! But it also pushed our batch processing into the

12-hour territory, totally unacceptable. And no, we could not run multiple batch jobs in parallel; they were meant to execute sequentially, and we were already pushing the database engine to its limits. Even if we could run several processes in parallel, it wouldn't shorten the time.

We clearly made an early design decision that wasn't scalable. We could not anticipate the need to scale this far – and no one could – but we allowed a critical scalability flow into our architecture, something we shouldn't have done, ever.

In the end, we partially solved the problem through software optimizations, and partially through expensive hardware upgrades. But the best part was – I learned my lesson.

<important>

Treat batch processing with respect, and avoid the batch design pattern entirely whenever possible, to keep the system infinitely scalable. If batch processing cannot be avoided, make it scale.

</important>

Let's revisit the reasons architects choose having batch processing in the first place:

- Because they are paying homage to the old tradition, or are forced to comply with pre-existing architecture decisions;
- As an attempt to speed up online transactions, by deferring non-essential portions of the work to a batch that runs at a later time;
- To decrease database contention at peak times, by deferring the work to night hours;
- To run periodic processing, such as producing hourly reports, or computing daily balances;
- To run processing at a specific time or date, such as producing a report each Sunday night.
- To move data to a data warehouse or to run other ETL (Extract, Transform and Load) workloads
- To perform statistical analysis
- To integrate with third party systems without an online API
- To re-index searchable data

By incorporating a batch job into the blueprint, we are potentially introducing a number of risks:

- Batch doesn't finish on time (runs too long, misses the allocated batch window);
- Batch doesn't run as planned (fails to start or crashes), having a debilitating effect on the next day's operations, which rely on the results of a nightly batch run;
- Multiple instances of a batch process are accidentally launched and run concurrently, while the batch code is not designed for concurrent execution;
- Batch crashes and is unsafe to re-start (will process a portion of the data twice);
- Batch accidentally runs the second time (will process all of the data twice);
- Batch runs in parallel with online transactions, and competes for resources (with the database being the most frequent point of contention);
- Periodic batch runs too long and doesn't finish before the beginning of the next scheduled run. Depending on the mechanism for launching batch jobs, a new instance of the batch may end up running concurrently with the previous one, or the new instance may not get launched at all.

Most of those risks can be mitigated through proper architecture and performance testing. However, I recommend to always look at the possibility of eliminating batch processing entirely. To that extent, the only valid reasons to have batch processing are:

- Periodic processing, i.e., the work that has to be performed every N minutes (or hours, or days).
- Scheduled processing, i.e., the work that has to be performed at a particular date & time, one-time or recurring[33].
- To integrate with third-party systems without an online API[34].

I intentionally excluded the use cases related to the database contention. In such cases, you must eliminate the root cause of the ailment – such as non-scalable database design – as opposed to prescribing bed rest and a pair of crutches. If your architecture needs an open-heart surgery, then the sooner you do it, the better.

---

[33] Scheduled processing can be potentially implemented as Periodic, by running frequently and checking the time. However, it represents a different use case, and is worth an independent consideration.

[34] This usually, but not always, falls into the scheduled processing category.

All other use cases can be implemented using the patterns described in this book, through asynchronous processing (see Latency in Chapter 7) and through event streaming (see Real-Time Processing and Event Streaming in Chapter 10).

When architecting a batch, try to follow the guidelines below, to avoid nasty surprises in the future.

Batch processes must be restartable. When processing transactions, mark those already processed. This way, you can skip the marked transactions if the batch is restarted, to avoid processing the same transaction more than once. If the batch follows a certain consistent order of processing, then you may use the *water level pattern* instead of marking individual transactions. For instance, if all transactions are sequentially numbered, you can record the latest number processed, and start from the next number on the subsequent run. This is a more efficient implementation, but it is harder to work with if multiple batch streams run concurrently, while marking individual transactions works well with concurrent batch execution. There are myriad of ways how these two algorithms can be applied to achieve an optimal implementation in each particular case.

Offload most of the work onto asynchronous processing. Identify transactions that require processing in the batch process, and then submit each transaction individually for processing by using event streaming. This allows to scale the processing of transactions and run them in parallel if the semantics of the batch permits out-of-order execution. The most typical batch process has a database query at the beginning, and then each result of the query can be submitted to a streaming engine and then processed by subscribed stream consumers. Partitioning of the stream and a higher number of consumers can be used to scale the processing part of the batch (but not the query).

Distribute the work between parallel processes. The goal here is to allow the batch scale through parallelism. Even if we offloaded the work through event streaming, we still have the query that needs to run fully at the beginning of the batch run. Sometimes, you can find a way to modify the query to allow different process instances pick different segments of data. The segmentation could be based on date, time, or a completely artificial characteristic. For instance, you can run three instances of a batch process concurrently, reporting on customers, having the first instance reporting all customers with (customerNumber % 3) == 0, the second instance with (customerNumber % 3) == 1, and third with (customerNumber % 3) == 2. Make sure parallelism is actually reducing the processing time; you may discover that you are creating a database contention resulting in completely opposite net effect from the one you seek.

The date or the time of the day when you run the batch should carry no semantic value. Let's consider this example. You must to produce a report on daily sales. The report must include all the sales transactions which took place on the previous day, until midnight. The batch which creates the report should not be required to run at midnight. It should be allowed to run at any time *after* midnight, and it must query all sales transactions from the database with the appropriate date and time filter. A good implementation of a sales report should accept the date or a range of dates as a parameter, allowing you to run it at any time in the future, and consistently produce the same result for the same parameter value.

Embrace failure. Just accept the inevitable: your batch will fail at some point. Make sure that crashes are (a) reported, (b) the batch continues if a single transaction failed, and (c) if an unusually large number of transactions fail then stop the batch and sound an alarm.

Observe the execution time. Monitor the time it takes for your batch process to run; compare the measured duration with the allocated batch time window. Sound an alarm if your batch takes longer than half of the allocated time – as a rule of thumb, you should be ready to process at least 2x of the projected volume. Ideally, you should have a scaling plan to reduce the time.

Create a telemetry feed. While your batch runs, you may not see if it is actually performing the work or just sits there deadlocked or waiting. Instrument your code with a telemetry feed, to enable monitoring. Create a dashboard showing current state of affairs. The most typical types of batch telemetry are:

- *proof of running*: a signal sent when the batch starts;
- *proof of finishing*: a signal sent when the batch finishes;
- *batch failure alert*: a signal sent when the batch crashes;
- *transaction failure alert*: a signal sent when an individual transaction fails;
- *heartbeat*: a signal sent every time the batch picks up a new transaction to process.

Avoid batch processing whenever you can. Offload as much work as possible through event streaming. Consider the possibility of scaling through a concurrent execution of multiple batch instances. Invest in error recovery. Closely monitor batch execution time. Create telemetry feeds.

https://anatoly.com/batch

CHAPTER 16
MULTI-TENANCY

> *If it's true that our species is alone in the universe, then I'd have to*
> *say the universe aimed rather low and settled for very little.*
> *– George Carlin*

In 2016, I was working on a marketing platform for wineries, breweries, and distilleries. The platform was capturing customer information as they visit a winery, and we were also placing a call to action on each bottle to trigger consumer engagement in retail stores. Each spirits brand had their own "universe", which was segregated from the others: they had their own database of customers, their own admin panel, analytics, and customer branding displayed to their customers.

The traditional thinking is that you can always run multiple instances of the system, using either different servers or different cloud accounts with different databases. Such an approach is called *physical segregation*, and it is very common in the software world. For instance, many companies run multiple environments for development, test, and production – usually using physical segregation. In some ways, physical segregation is the ultimate solution, because it not only allows you to create a "walled garden" for each environment but also can run different versions of the software in each. This is leveraged by many companies in their dev/test/prod deployment workflows.

However, many SaaS (Software as a Service) offerings require a very lightweight segregation between the customers, since running physically segregated environments for each customer is cost prohibitive and operationally challenging. For SaaS, software architects usually employ *logical segregation,* i.e., the type of architecture which allows for multiple customers, or *tenants*, to share the entire infrastructure and code base, while being logically independent from the others. With proper architecture, the customers are unable to tell if their account is powered by a dedicated instance of the system, or if they are sharing resources with the others. Such architecture is called *multi-tenant*. Each customer in such architecture is a *tenant*.

It is important not to confuse the tenants and the end users. In the SaaS world, tenants are usually businesses which purchased a service subscription, while users are individuals who work in those businesses, or end customers of those businesses. For instance, your company may purchase a CRM subscription – let's say a cloud-based SalesForce solution – then SalesForce treats your company as a tenant in their cloud, while you and other employees of your company are the users with the access to the solution. The users of the same tenant are not segregated, they are accessing the shared database of CRM contacts and tickets, but no one from your company can access the data from another tenant of SalesForce cloud.

When building a multi-tenant system, the most common approach is to add the identity of the tenant to the primary key in every database table, creating a logical segregation from the get-go. This generally works, but you may need to do more when it comes to consumption of external services and other interactions with the outside world. Imagine you built a CRM, and one of your tenants sends spam emails, which can get your domain blacklisted, negatively affecting all your customers. Or imagine you integrate with an SMS provider, and one of the tenants sends millions of messages, clogging your SMS delivery queue across all customers? Do you need to segregate logging? These are just a few of the questions you must be asking yourself while building a real-world multi-tenant solution.

But what if you have no need to be multi-tenant? The need for multi-tenancy in SaaS solutions is obvious, but what if you are an e-commerce company, and you are architecting your system to power your own business, no more, no less? The answer is – you don't know what the future might bring. On many occasions, I saw e-commerce companies create a new brand name to address another segment of the market. The difference between the existing brand and the new one is mainly in branding and go to market strategy, and they don't share the customer database. When this happens, the companies with single-tenant architecture are forced into deploying multiple instances of the system, which is usually costly not only because of the need for additional hardware, but because now the operations team has two systems to monitor and maintain. There are also other reasons to have multi-tenancy – for testing new product rollouts and for the demos, to mention just a few.

Back to my marketing platform for wine and spirits. I was approached in 2018 with a request from a large and very desirable prospect to create a clone of my system for their purposes. The prospect wanted to re-sell the services offered by my platform in a different market, under their own name. My implementation of the multi-tenancy model was designed for segregation of the customers but shared all the internal tooling such as customer service and billing, as well as connections to third party vendors. This prevented me from bringing the new prospect up on the infrastructure which was already in place. I could only offer them a standalone instance of the system. But the cost of operating a new instance made the deal economically unviable, and the it fell through. This happened because my architecture only considered customer-facing multi-tenancy but wasn't multi-tenant on the back-end. The most straightforward solution to such problem is to allow grouping of customers, each group having its own ops tools and dashboards. In the most flexible implementation, the groups may overlap. It is also important to make such groupings configurable, in anticipation of future changes.

The diagram below illustrates the potential complexity of data segregation in multi-tenant systems:

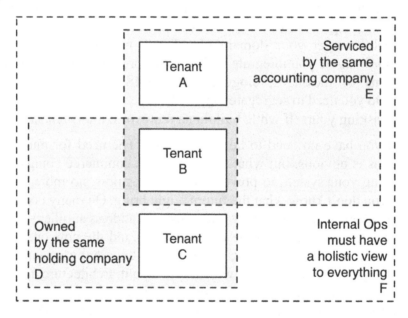

Here, we have three tenants A, B, and C with a definitive need to have their data segregated. However, tenants A and B are serviced by the same accounting company E, and that company must have access to the data of A and B. Further, tenants B and C are owned by the same holding company, and the owners must have access to the data of B and C. You are the operator of the entire system (F) and must have access to everything.

The data segregation between A, B, and C is usually built into the data model. However, I wouldn't recommend doing the same for D and E. One day, tenant B may get sold to another owner, and the relationships built into the persistent data could be hard to update. This can be fixed by having *access control lists* (*ACLs*) to map access for D and E to the tenants. We covered ACLs briefly when discussing authorization aspects of APIs (Chapter 14).

It is important to implement your own access (F) through ACLs as well. This way, you will not repeat my mistake of giving internal dashboards unlimited access to everything.

A word of warning: ACLs may come with significant performance penalties where it comes to retrieving long sorted collections of data. For instance, retrieving a list of all customers from the database visible to the holding company D requires retrieval of all customer records for B and C, and then sorting of the entire list. With the large number of customers, this can take a long time, and may consume a lot of resources. One of the solutions is to create indexing of data based on both the desired sort order and the ACLs and rebuild those indexes when ACLs change. It is easier to build indexing when ACLs are attached to user roles and not specific users – this way, you end up maintaining indexes per role, and not per user, significantly reducing the amount of indexing work.

<tldr>

Consider making your architecture multi-tenant, even if you see no immediate application for it. Multi-tenancy goes beyond customer-facing features, all the way to third party vendors and the internal operations.

https://anatoly.com/multi-tenancy

</tldr>

CHAPTER 17
UNBLOCK CODING AND TESTING

Some national parks have long waiting lists for camping reservations. When you have to wait a year to sleep next to a tree, something is wrong.

— George Carlin

A few years back, I've taken on a job of managing a cross-functional engineering team, responsible for retrofitting the existing e-commerce and manufacturing solution with new products and services. The engineers on the team knew their trade well, have been with the company for a while, and I wasn't expecting any big surprises. The very first month on the job has proven me wrong when one of the ongoing projects came to a screeching halt. There was no warning shot. Simply, one day, at the daily standup meeting, one engineer (let's call him Steve) simply announced:

"I am blocked!"

"What do you mean, Steve?" I asked incredulously.

"My work is dependent on the component which is not coded yet. The component is a responsibility of another team. I already talked to them, and they promised to have it ready it in two days. Until then, I can work on something else."

I didn't like this. Two days could easily turn into a week, and by the time Steve gets back to his task, he would have no recollection of what he was working on, and the overall project timeline will shift.

"Is there a way you could mock the missing implementation and continue?" I asked.

Now it was Steve's turn to look at me weirdly.

"How do you mean *mock*?"

"Well, *emulate*, create a dummy implementation of the interface which does nothing for real but can be called from your code – so that you can finish coding, build it, and test to the extent possible?"

I drew a blank stare in return. Another engineer was blocked the next day. And two more the day after. Something was very wrong… and I was having the worst case of déjà vu I've ever had.

The thing is – I saw this before, in early 1990s, when I was on the team developing financial software in COBOL. The language lacked the modern syntactical sugar, didn't support interfaces or OOP, and SOLID principles were yet to be formulated. We were on the clock to deliver the software in a very tight timeframe. We created a highly optimized waterfall development plan which meticulously tracked every component dependency, to make sure that we could build the system from the ground up without waiting on unfinished components. Our project manager was spending all her time rearranging the waterfall execution plan on daily basis, and still, some tasks would take longer than expected, blocking a few developers every now and then. This was a true nightmare from the past, the one I put behind 25 years earlier… and I was facing it again, in the brave new world of agile project execution! Only this time, there was no project manager tracking dependencies – the team was running agile weekly sprints without prioritization or dependency tracking of the tasks.

As it turned out, the team was used to assemble fully functional software, without ever resorting to abstractions. The engineers expected all code dependencies to be fully functional before they start coding a new component. To illustrate this, consider a snippet from a hypothetical e-commerce system which places an order for a single product:

```
<code>
  import { collectPayment } from './accounting';
  import { submitShipment } from './delivery';
  import { placeOrder } from './ecomm';
  import { User } from './user';

  export const checkout = ( customer : User ) : void => {

    ...
    let orderNumber = placeOrder( customer );
    let totalAmount = collectPayment( customer );
    let trackingNumber = submitShipment( customer );
    ...

  };
</code>
```

Now, your task is to add an email notification, sent to the customer once the order is placed. You could do it like this:

```
<code>
import { collectPayment } from './accounting';
import { submitShipment } from './delivery';
import { placeOrder } from './ecomm';
import { User } from './user';
import { sendEmail } from './notifications';

export const checkout = ( customer : User ) : void => {

  ...
  let orderNumber = placeOrder( customer );
  let totalAmount = collectPayment( customer );
  let trackingNumber = submitShipment( customer );
  let emailSubject = `Your order is on its way!`;
  let emailBody = `Congratulations, ${ customer.name }!\n`
                + `Your order #{orderNumber} has shipped.\n`
                + `You can track it via USPS\n`
                + `Your tracking number is ${ trackingNumber }`;
  sendEmail( customer.emailAddress, emailSubject, emailBody );

  ...
};
</code>
```

And this is a correct approach... but there is one little problem: the `notifications` library is a responsibility of another team, and it is not ready yet. They promise it to be ready in 2 days... or 3... Meanwhile, you can't use `sendEmail()` function; it doesn't exist – and you are *blocked*! Or are you?

How about spending a few minutes and creating a simple emulator for the `sendEmail()` function? Let's have a look:

```
<code>
import { collectPayment } from './accounting';
import { submitShipment } from './delivery';
import { placeOrder } from './ecomm';
import { User } from './user';

//TODO: uncomment the line below when the 'notifications' package is ready
//import { sendEmail } from './notifications';

//TODO: delete the function below when the 'notifications' package is ready
const sendEmail = (
  emailAddress : string,
  emailSubject : string,
  emailBody: string
) : void => {
  console.log(
```

```
    `emulated sendEmail() to ${ emailAddress }:\n`
    + `${ emailSubject }\n${ emailBody }`
  );
};
export const checkout = ( customer : User ) : void => {
  ...
  let orderNumber = placeOrder( customer );
  let totalAmount = collectPayment( customer );
  let trackingNumber = submitShipment( customer );
  let emailSubject = `Your order is on its way!`;
  let emailBody = `Congratulations, ${ customer.name }!\n`
                  + `Your order #{orderNumber} has shipped.\n`
                  + `You can track it via USPS\n`
                  + `Your tracking number is ${ trackingNumber }`;
  sendEmail( customer.emailAddress, emailSubject, emailBody );
  ...
};
```
</code>

Now we can write and test the code, and the only thing left is to address the TODO items in the code, once the notifications library is ready.

If this feels way too trivial, I agree wholeheartedly. In real life, however, the number of interdependencies between modules is much larger, and developers cannot emulate all their dependencies all by themselves. Besides, there could be other modules that require sendEmail() functionality, and we don't want all the developers spend their time reinventing the wheel over and over again. Instead, I recommend embracing emulation of components as an approach to software architecture.

Let's consider the same example. When we create the architecture for the notifications module, we first create an interface that embodies the contract of that module. For instance, consider the following notifications-defs:

<code>
```
// module notifications-defs.ts

export interface Notifications {
  sendEmail(
    emailAddress : string,
    emailSubject : string,
    emailBody : string
  ) : void;
}
```
</code>

We also create an *emulator implementation* in `notifications-emu`:

```
// module notifications-emu.ts

import { Notifications } from './notifications-defs';

export class NotificationsEmulator implements Notifications {
  sendEmail(
    emailAddress : string,
    emailSubject : string,
    emailBody : string
  ) : void {
    console.log(
      `emulated sendEmail() to ${ emailAddress }:\n`
      + `${ emailSubject }\n${ emailBody }`
    );
  }
};
```

At this point, the architect's work is done, and developers take over. Let's assume that development of `notification` module is not due for another week. However, we don't have to wait, and can code `checkout` right away, like this:

```
// module checkout.ts

import { collectPayment } from './accounting';
import { submitShipment } from './delivery';
import { placeOrder } from './ecomm';
import { User } from './user';
import { Notifications } from './notifications-defs';

export const checkout = ( notifications : Notifications, customer : User ) :
void => {

  ...
  let orderNumber = placeOrder( customer );
  let totalAmount = collectPayment( customer );
  let trackingNumber = submitShipment( customer );
  let emailSubject = `Your order is on its way!`;
  let emailBody = `Congratulations, ${ customer.name }!\n`
                + `Your order #{orderNumber} has shipped.\n`
                + `You can track it via USPS\n`
                + `Your tracking number is ${ trackingNumber }`;
  notifications.sendEmail( customer.emailAddress, emailSubject, emailBody );

  ...
};
```

As you can see, `checkout.ts` no longer depends on having `sendEmail()` implemented for real, and can be filly coded. No one gets blocked!

But how do we test it? Let's create a rudimentary[35] test for `checkout()`:

```
import { Notifications } from './notifications-defs';
import { NotificationsEmulator } from './notifications-emu';
import { User } from './user';
import { checkout } from './checkout';

const notifications : Notifications = new NotificationsEmulator();

const customer : User = {
  name : `Anatoly`,
  emailAddress : `contact@anatoly.com`
};

checkout( notifications, customer );
```

Now, we can both write the checkout code, and also test it! If we wanted to, we could add more test cases, and we use an off-the-shelf testing framework to run them and check results. With this, we unblocked not only the development team but also the QA team to create unit tests. With the use of emulators, you can structure your project to have the tests created before developers start coding the real implementation. This is known as *test-first approach* to software development. With this, developers can verify their work immediately, by running the tests created in advance. If you develop test-first, then the quality of the code your team produces goes sky-high.

One of my book's reviewers, while reading this, said: "But this is just standard dependency injection. You've already covered this earlier in the book!" Yes, the mechanism in use is indeed the dependency injection. And we could take it a step further and use inversion of control pattern to configure the instantiation of implementation classes (emulators vs real) via a configuration file. But that's not the point. The point is this: as an architect, *create emulators for each component alongside with their interfaces*. Alternatively, have your team code *all* emulators before the "real" development starts. Having emulators enables almost infinite parallelism for development process, i.e., you will be able to create any number of workstreams for your project, without dependencies, and without anyone getting

---

[35] A real-life test is a bit more complex, it must have a way of checking the results of the test execution.

blocked. It also allows you to practice test-first development and paves way for a smooth execution of your agile sprints. Conversely, not doing this will likely plunge your team into the dark ages of waterfall planning, poorly tested software, and missed deadlines.

In the ideal world, you should be able to assemble the entire system from emulators first. Then, you build a plan for replacing those emulators with real code. Some pieces of functionality can remain emulated until later phases, potentially months after the first version of the system goes into production. For instance, you may decide to release an MVP (minimal viable product) version of your software which doesn't send notifications emails when an order is placed. However, you can have an emulator in place, "reserving" the spot for sending emails, which you will implement once you have the resources to do so. Meanwhile, the system will remain fully functional. When the time comes, your developers will simply swap the implementation of the emulator with the real thing, which is best done through a configuration file, by using inversion of control. This will also allow you to turn features on and off at will, differently in test and production environments, running the same version of the software.

Not all emulators can be implemented with a simplistic dependency injection. You must be able to emulate APIs, datastore, UI components, and more. The APIs can be emulated via direct calls, datastore by storing everything in memory, UI components could be all gray rectangles submitting hard-coded data instead of real input, etc.

<tldr>

Create emulators alongside with interfaces. Embrace the test-first approach to development. See the light.

https://anatoly.com/unblock

</tldr>

CHAPTER 18
RUNTIME INFRASTRUCTURE

Electricity is really just organized lightning.
– George Carlin

The question of runtime infrastructure is frequently overlooked when architecting a solution – and more often than not, the finalized architecture inherently limits your choices. When speaking of the infrastructure, I loosely refer to *servers, networks, software components, and cloud services required to run your system.*

Many engineers buy into the promise of "just doing microservices" or "just doing containers" or "just planning to provision servers", and move on with development, leaving the business to later discover all the hidden but significant costs associated with running, deploying, and supporting the system, beyond the "pure" engineering costs. Will your infrastructure require a human to manage? Will you need a fully staffed DevOps/SRE team to support your operations? How much will it cost to run the system at full scale? Can you save $$ while you are running the proof of concept for the first 6 months before you get funded? How costly will it be to handle the occasional traffic spikes? How well will your system protect the customer's data? How can you best support the future development and testing efforts?

Most of these questions are answered by selecting your hosting model. Several options exist:

- Use your own dedicated hardware
- Provision dedicated hardware from a cloud provider
- Provision virtual hardware from a cloud provider
- Install a container solution on dedicated or virtual hardware
- Rely on fully managed container orchestration solution
- Go serverless

Let's have a look at each option individually[36].

---

[36] In complex cases, you may end up combining several hosting solutions in one system.

Use your own dedicated hardware. This is the most involving option – and this is what every company was doing in the past, before the cloud providers. This means building your own server farm, ensuring redundancy and security, servicing hardware when necessary, etc. Very involving and very costly, both to build and to operate. Why would you do it nowadays? If your business requires specialized server hardware, peripherals or connections, which are unavailable from cloud providers, then this is for you. Other use cases include applications which must comply with government-imposed security regulations, systems which must be physically disconnected from the Internet, or applications which exchange excessive amounts of data with existing on-premises servers. For the vast majority of business applications, however, this option is too expensive and inefficient to be even considered.

Provision dedicated hardware from a cloud provider. The only times when you may need truly dedicated hardware is when running real-time workflows, or continuously performing heavy computations. In those cases, context switching performed by virtualization software negatively affects performance, and you may want to have the hardware allocated 100% to your workflows. This is also rare in the business application world, but more common in big data analytics and in real-time applications (GPS navigation, robotics, air traffic control, live video processing.)

Provision virtual hardware from a cloud provider. This is one of the most popular options today (although not necessarily the most optimal one). This option is great because many cloud providers allow you to dynamically scale the number of your virtual servers as your sustained load changes. For instance, you can configure a dynamic load balancer to automatically increase or decrease the capacity (number of virtual servers) based on the average number of requests received per hour. This will save you money, in contrast with provisioning for the maximum capacity required and paying for the low-load intervals as much as you do for the high-load ones.

With both dedicated and virtual hardware, most cloud providers allow you to pre-create images of your server hard drives and then launch new server instances using those images by either making an API call or by specifying auto-scaling rules. A good example of such service is Amazon Elastic Compute Cloud, aka EC2. EC2 allows you to create server images and provides you with a web-based console to manage your instances manually, and with an API to do so programmatically. You can also use Elastic Load Balancer service (ELB) to automatically scale a pool of servers up and down, depending on the specified set of rules.

Install a container solution on dedicated or virtual hardware. An alternative to deploying your app to virtual servers is using Docker containers. Docker is a set of tools for packaging your application or its independent components, for later deployment to a container framework, such as Docker Swarm or Kubernetes. Using Docker streamlines deployment and management of application components, by creating an abstraction for manipulating components[37]. Components packaged using Docker usually expose HTTP-based APIs, serve web pages over HTTP, or implement batch workloads. Depending on the container framework, using Docker may sometimes limit your load balancing abilities, when compared to the advanced balancing solutions available directly from a cloud provider. The challenge in workload balancing with Docker is that it introduces two levels of load balancing. The first level of balancing works with Docker container instances, within the capacity limits of the provisioned hardware. The second level of balancing works with the hardware itself. The most commonly used solution is to maintain a single Docker instance per virtual server instance, and balance servers using the dynamic load balancing available from the cloud provider. This works, although not optimally.

Rely on a fully managed container orchestration solution. Some challenges of managing and load-balancing both hardware and Docker instances are alleviated by fully managed services provided by some of the cloud providers. One example is Amazon's Elastic Kubernetes Service (EKS) which is fully compatible with standalone Kubernetes deployments, but is tightly integrated with Amazon Cloud infrastructure and allows you to take advantage of several built-in load balancing and scaling algorithms.

Up until now, the options we considered were imposing only minor limitations on your technology stack, because we were dealing with servers, dedicated or virtual, and we remained in full control of what gets installed on those servers[38]. This changes as we move to the serverless option described below, which offers you to trade some of the freedom for simplicity and cost.

---

[37] Lots of effort has been going lately into standardization of containerization solutions. For more information, check out Open Container Initiative (OCI) at opencontainers.org

[38] One notable exception is Docker, which limits your choice of the OS, and this in turn affects the rest of the software stack, unless it is completely OS-agnostic.

Go serverless. This one is my personal favorite. A good example of serverless cloud services combines two services available from Amazon Cloud: Lambda and API Gateway. Lambda allows you to deploy pure code, without thinking of the infrastructure at all, in a highly scalable manner. The cloud automatically manages the hardware necessary for deployment of your Lambda code, and automatically scales your deployment by running as many Lambda instances as the number of concurrent requests coming in. API Gateway, in turn, publishes your API and web endpoints, and routes the incoming requests to your Lambda code. What you are getting, in the end, is a *near-limitless compute capacity which runs your code concurrently, scaling automatically*. Since creation of Lambda instances is lightweight, it is significantly faster than a virtual server or a docker instance warmup. For that reason, Lambdas scale extremely fast, usually fast enough to quickly respond to traffic spikes. With servers or Docker instances, you are forced to maintain certain "warm" capacity to take on the spikes, which means you pay for the hardware while it is not being fully utilized between the spikes. With Lambda, you pay for the execution time you consume, which makes it more economical in many cases.

Consider an extreme example. You are building a startup, which has to reliably process e-commerce transactions. You expect 100 purchases per day for the first 6 months. Each purchase takes 1 second of compute time, so 100 purchases x 30 days x 6 months takes 18,000 seconds, or 5 hours total of compute time. If you go with traditional server architecture, then you pay for 2 servers (for redundancy) x 24 hours x 30 days x 6 months = 8,640 hours. That's 1,728 times more compute time than you actually need!

Now imagine another exaggerated example: you are running a TV ad, offering a deep limited-time discount. Once the ad is displayed, all the interested viewers flock to your web site, approximately at the same time. Your site offers them a customized all-inclusive quote based on the options selected and the zip code entered. Let's say your ad runs 10 times a day, for 30 days, and generates around 1,000,000 quotes from each run. With Lambda, your monthly cost of calculating quotes is the cost of handling 300,000,000 requests. Assuming you run the most expensive Lambda configuration (maximum memory and maximum performance), and assuming 1 second of compute time spent per request, this will cost you approximately $0.00005[39] per request, or $15,000 monthly. If you use servers instead, you must have enough capacity in place to manage the traffic spike when

---

[39] This pricing listed here and below is as of September 2019; check the latest on AWS web site.

the ad runs. For simplicity, let's say each server can process 4 quotes concurrently. This means you must provision 1,000,000 / 4 = 250,000 servers – a totally absurd number. A virtual server with equivalent to the quoted Lambda capacity costs upwards of $200 monthly, bringing the monthly total to $50,000,000. *Give it some time to sink in: $15,000 using Lambda and $50,000,000 using servers.* Of course, this example is an intentional exaggeration, but it nicely illustrates the point: if you have spiky traffic, then serverless architecture is likely to be far more cost effective than traditional server allocations[40].

Serverless implementations have their inherent limitations. For instance, AWS Lambda limits you to the maximum size of request/response of 6mb, available memory of 3GB, max execution time of 15 min, max code size of 250MB, max disk space of 512MB, and max concurrency of 3,000 Lambdas running in parallel (in the U.S. data centers)[41].

These limitations usually prevent you from running batch workloads using AWS Lambda, unless your batch jobs can finish their work or enqueue all the tasks for asynchronous execution in under 15 minutes. Amazon Cloud has another service called AWS Batch which helps to work around this particular limitation.

You also must consider the future traffic volume and patterns. If you expect a shift from spiky traffic to significant sustained loads over time, then you must do the math and ensure that the cost of a serverless deployment remains competitive to a server- or container-based approach. You may also consider a hybrid solution or eventual migration from serverless to server-based – but in either case, this type of analysis and planning must go into the foundation of your architecture.

The maximum benefit of serverless infrastructure is achieved if your entire system is architected around *fully managed services*. Under fully managed I mean services which are managed by a third party, thus requiring little to no attention on your part. For instance, AWS Lambda is a fully managed hosting service, where you need not worry about the actual servers; a fully managed database like DynamoDB doesn't require you to monitor and optimize disk space, memory, partitioning, replication, etc. At the end of the day, most companies are not in the business of building and managing technology infrastructure – they provide services to the end

---

[40] In real life, you spike load will spread over a short period of time, say 5 minutes, making the realistic numbers about 300 times lower. This brings your server count down to around 800, and your monthly cost to $160,000. Still, it's an order of magnitude difference in hardware costs alone.
[41] Those limits are subject to change; check the latest AWS documentation for the most current.

consumers – yet many spend significant $$ on managing their own servers, databases, streaming engines, and container frameworks. The cost drivers here are not only the infrastructure itself but the cost of the team that plans, builds, and then supports it.

Amazon did a great job providing a range of fully managed services, and I had a great success building system on top of 100% fully managed AWS infrastructure.

<tldr>

The choice of your hosting model, or the ability to move between select models, is one of the most pivotal architectural decisions where it comes to scalability and operating costs. The costs are not limited to the hardware and services but also include the labor to deploy and maintain the system. The simplicity of delivering code to your infrastructure also affects stability of your software releases and your readiness for Continuous Integration and Continuous Delivery (CI/CD).

https://anatoly.com/runtime-infrastructure

</tldr>

CHAPTER 19
RUNTIME FRAMEWORKS

Never underestimate the power of stupid people in large groups.
– George Carlin

The purpose of runtime frameworks (let's call them simply *frameworks*) is to speed up the software development process. The frameworks are usually produced by third parties, frequently open source, although you can develop some of your own. Most of the frameworks are general purpose and can be used for a wide variety of application domains (or so they claim). Some frameworks pack significant amount of complex code and algorithms, and some create standards extension by third party developers – both of which can save you tons of time and money.

For instance, here are some of the popular frameworks for business application development in Java:

- Hibernate: enables object-relational mapping (ORM) for your data model
- Spring: enterprise app development
- Vaadin: web app development
- Google Web Toolkit (GWT): web development in Java
- Java Server Faces (JSF): building UI from reusable components
- Spark: unified analytics for big data
- Flink: stateful computations over data streams
- Beam: massively parallel processing of data streams
- Angular: building single-page web UI
- React: building highly interactive web UI

Most language-specific frameworks are distributed as code libraries, which are then bundled with your application. Such frameworks are usually tightly integrated with your programming language for maximum performance (Hibernate, Spring, Vaadin, GTW, JSF).

Language-neutral frameworks are usually installed separately server-side, and work with your application through a set of APIs, usually HTTP-based (Beam).

Frameworks are double-edged swords. Selecting the right ones for the job will save you the time and money. Conversely, poor choices may lead to significant losses in productivity and operational risks.

The relationship you form with a framework and the team behind it is asymmetric. You make a serious long-term commitment to the framework, while the framework's creators usually make no commitment to you whatsoever. If the framework shows its flaws late in the game, you are likely to incur considerable time and cost overruns replacing or fixing it. Keep in mind that the authors of the framework created it to solve their own problems, not yours. Unless you know with certainty that the framework is built to address the needs of the application domain which substantially overlaps with yours, the risk of adopting a framework is incredibly high.

Regardless of which frameworks you choose, delay your decision until everything else in your architecture is fully fleshed out. Frameworks should be the last choice you make. Never allow a framework to define your architecture. Figure out your entire architecture first, and only then decide on how to implement it faster by incorporating an existing framework.

Also, for each of the frameworks which you are eyeballing, think twice if you actually need it. Many frameworks do just a little tiny bit of additional automation but will forever confine you in its sometimes-limiting paradigm. Make sure the framework gives you significant long-term value without putting you into a straitjacket.

Whatever the choices of frameworks you make, treat them as replaceable. To achieve that, do not allow any framework dependencies to penetrate your code base. This can be achieved by abstracting the frameworks using interfaces, and making your code depend on those interfaces. Concrete implementations call frameworks directly and are supplied to your code using Dependency Injection pattern, or – better – by specifying concrete implementations in a configuration file using Inversion of Control pattern. This way, your codebase remains framework-neutral, and you avoid a potential vendor lock-in.

This approach is more actionable for server-side frameworks, and less realistic for client-side. UI frameworks usually force you into their component and event propagation model, thus creating the scaffolding for you to put your code into. Such frameworks are extremely hard to replace without rewriting the entire view implementation.

Don't make your architecture choices dependent on a framework. Frameworks must significantly simplify and accelerate coding. Do not allow frameworks to penetrate your code base.

https://anatoly.com/runtime-frameworks

CHAPTER 20
BRAINSTORMING

Life gets really simple once you cut out all the bullshit they teach you in school.

– George Carlin

In 2009, I went on building a social marketing platform. It was intended to become a groundbreaking solution, both technologically and functionally. The social media space was evolving fast, and I had to move even faster to keep up with the market. I hired a good engineering team, all seasoned developers.

When brainstorming the architecture, the team quickly dismissed the options they knew to be overly complex and expensive and narrowed the decision making down to one very reasonable proposal. It wasn't a jewel, but we all knew it will work for our purposes.

It worked quite well indeed, up until the moment a few years later, when we moved towards serverless cloud architecture. Then we discovered that the transition would cost us an arm and a leg, mainly due to the shortcuts in the architecture we'd taken.

Even more discouraging was the realization we saved very little by dismissing the more complex options early on. By excluding them from the overall analysis process, we did not see the benefits we could have ripped in other parts of the system. A quick calculation has shown that, had we kept all the options on the table, we would have saved the time and money in the long term – and our later transition to serverless would have been a breeze.

This is when I realized that eliminating any of the ideas that come up early on is a systemic mistake and should be avoided, no matter how obvious or appealing such elimination might seem. Naturally, it turned out that I was not the first to identify this problem; there exists a business process which addresses the issue perfectly. The process was originally invented at the most unlikely of all places – the Walt Disney Studios—and is called **The Disney Method**. Here is how it works.

Imagine three rooms, occupied by three teams.

The first room is occupied by the *Dreamers*. The Dreamers generate ideas, with no limitations or judgment, no matter how bold or absurd those ideas might seem. Nothing is censored. Nothing is too absurd or silly. All things are possible for a Dreamer. At Walt Disney Studios, the Dreamers create ideas for new motion pictures. The work of the Dreamers is recorded and once a *dream* (a movie) is fully conceived, it is then passed to the second room.

The second room is occupied by the *Realists*. The Realists consider each dream and create an execution plan for it. They think of the technologies that might be required, an execution plan, resources, budget, schedule, etc. The Realists create their execution plan without constraining themselves with cost or complexity of the execution. They may propose multiple plans for executing the same dream. The plans proposed by Realists are also recorded, and then passed on to the third room.

The third room is occupied by the *Critics*. The Critics review all the implementation plans created by the Realists and try to punch holes in them by playing devil's advocates. Their main concerns are time, budget, resources, risks, legality, public opinion, customer satisfaction, reusability, etc. It is important to note that the Critics are instructed to criticize the execution plan created by the Realists, but not the original Dream. The Dream is untouchable. However, a connection should be made between the elements of the original idea, the respective parts of the implementation plan, and the criticism. This creates the necessary feedback for the Dreamers to iterate on their ideas going forward.

If the Critics fail to generate significant criticism for an implementation plan, then the plan is ready to be executed. At Walt Disney Studios, this means they move forward shooting the motion picture.

If, however, the Critics provided a significant amount of criticism for the plan, then the whole recorded Dream+Plan+Criticism package is sent back to the first room with the Dreamers. The Dreamers review the feedback, and either (a) ditch the original idea entirely, or (b) modify the original idea, and send it through another iteration with the Realists and the Critics.

The process repeats itself until the idea is ready for implementation, or until it is tabled until another time. At Disney, some movie ideas had to wait until the inception of the computer graphics.

The diagram below illustrates the Disney Method:

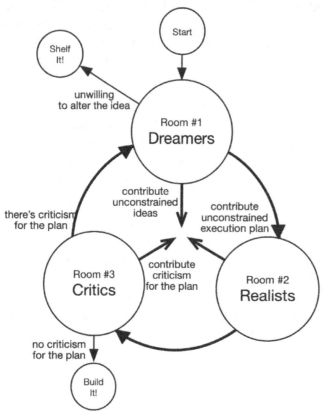

But of course, we are not here to shoot a movie; we are software architects. Let consider the adaptation of the Disney Method to the process of developing software architecture. For us, the dream represents the full unconstrained business specification for the product or service; the execution plan is the software architecture, and the criticism combines all business and technical flaws of the architecture, including its complexity, cost, risks, and time to market.

We can depict the process as follows:

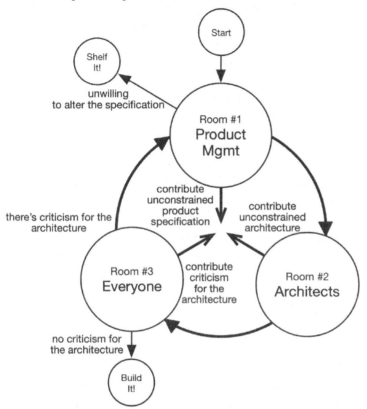

Let's look at it more closely. First, product management (or the entrepreneur who takes on that role) are asked to come up with the ideal product they can think of, without constraining themselves by any concerns related to cost or time or personnel or anything else. All they focus on is what the product should be, if they can have it all. That ideal product is expressed in a form of a written specification; it's the "dream". It is then passed to the team of architects (or a single architect/developer in a smaller configuration). The architects map out the architecture for implementing the spec, without constraining themselves with time, cost, or available resources. They cut no corners, and come up with the best architecture possible, and document it – and it becomes the "plan". Then, everyone (product managers, architects, developers, and everyone else who can meaningfully contribute) familiarize themselves with the architecture and begin criticizing it from various angles – cost, time, etc. The proposed product is never criticized, only the architecture. In the process, the architects help connecting the dots between the most heavily criticized architectural decisions and the elements of the product specification which led to those decisions in the first place. If no meaningful critique has been generated, then the product is ready to be built. If there is critique, then all the gathered information is passed back to the product management, and they can decide if they want to shelf their idea entirely, or if they want to drop or alter some of the features which are responsible for the most criticized parts of the architecture. If they decide to revise the specification, then the altered product spec is re-submitted, and the process repeats itself.

You are not required to physically have the three rooms, as long as your process has the three steps of the method clearly separated. You aren't required to have different individuals performing the roles of Dreamers, Critics and Realists either. You can wear those three hats all by yourself, or you can distribute the roles within your team – as long as you never wear two hats at once, and give yourself enough time to clearly switch the context and fully slip into the new role before participating in the process[42]. The key is to fully associate yourself with one role at a time and to strictly follow the guidelines. No early or partial criticism, no shortcuts, no attempts to avoid complexity. Aim for a perfect architecture for a perfect product, and you shall have it!

<tldr>

Use the Disney Method to fully flesh out both the "dream" and the plan that brings it to life. Never criticize the dream, only criticize the plan. Criticism shall be based on the holistic view of the entire plan and shall not be intermixed with the creative steps.

https://anatoly.com/brainstorming

</tldr>

---

[42] If you are having hard time switching roles in the Disney Method, then you may want to check out the Disassociation techniques in Neuro-Linguistic Programming (NLP).

WHERE DO WE GO FROM HERE?

Standing ovations have become far too commonplace. What we need are ovations where the audience members all punch and kick one another.

– George Carlin

I hope you enjoyed reading this book as much as I enjoyed writing it. If you made the effort to understand the principles, then you should be ready to take your software architecture work to the entirely new level. But, per Confucius, *knowledge without practice is useless; practice without knowledge is dangerous.* You just acquired the new knowledge. Put it to use right away, while it is still fresh in your head. If you have a project at work which needs architecture, great. Otherwise, start tinkering in your own free time. Or do both. Once you solidify your understanding in the form of actual blueprints and code, you will possess the real-life experience, propelling your career to the next level and de-risking your entrepreneurial endeavors.

Now, what about the promise of becoming an awesome software architect? You should feel some awesomeness already: getting through this book wasn't an easy feat. But our journey isn't over yet. On the contrary, it's just the beginning… I have more topics to share, enough for one or two books to come. I've already started working on Book 2. Here is the list of topics I am planning to cover, not necessarily in this order:

- Embracing immutability. Pure functions. Defensive programming.
- Lazy execution. Declarative vs imperative programming.
- Localization. Multi-lingual implementations. Multiple currencies and other localization considerations.
- Date and Time. Servicing customers across time zones. DST. Date and time intervals. Calendar calculations. Proper persistence of time vs calendar values.
- Reliable scheduling without batch processing. Customer journeys.
- Exception and error handling.
- Worldwide service delivery. Multi-region deployments. CDN edge deployments.

- Audit trails. "Explain mode" for complex calculations and decision making.
- Push Messaging. Browser-based and mobile push. Real-time customer interactions: chatting, sharing, liking.
- Asset and content management. Content delivery.
- Embracing video. On-demand video. Video streaming. Interactive video.
- Source control. Massively parallel development. Release management. Deployment strategies. Continuous Integration and Continuous Deployment and Delivery (CI/CD).
- Testable architectures. Testing and troubleshooting pipelines. Separate environments for development, test, staging and production. Data management across environments.
- Turning new features on and off. Killswitch vs IoC. Functional dependencies.
- UX and UI best practices. Reusable UI Components. Accommodating all display sizes.
- Landing pages and funnels. User workflows that sell. Product-specific user workflows. Fluid UI.
- A/B testing. Conversion funnels. Behavioral analytics.
- Capacity planning. Load/Stress testing.
- Data security. Privacy considerations. Handling of personally identifiable information (PII). GDPR compliance.
- Development of Domain-Specific Languages (DSLs).
- Product setup. Multi-dimensional products and services. Customizable products. Testability of complex products.
- Business Workflows. Building flexible workflows. Combining human and machine tasks in the same workflows. State machines.
- Common Business Intelligence (BI) data models and implementation patterns.
- Modernization of legacy systems. Retrofitting vs integrating vs rewriting. Gradual transitioning.
- Serverless architecture patterns in AWS. Building applications quickly using fully managed components (DynamoDB, SQS, Kinesis, Lambda, CloudWatch, S3, API Gateway, Certificate Manager, Route 53, IAM).
- Immediate vs Eventual consistency. Non-transactional distributed systems.
- Roadmap planning. Project management. Agile, waterfall, and combined planning and tracking. Estimates. MVPs. Risk management.
- Team building. Leadership. Technical mentorship. Useful elements of NLP. On-premises vs remote teams. Outsourcing.

Which topics I should be getting your way first? Which additional topics would you like me to cover? I'd like to hear from you!

https://anatoly.com/feedback-architect-1

</tldr>

Last but not least: I would love to hear your honest opinion about this book. Please *rate and review it on Amazon*; this will help other readers like you. I thank you in advance for your feedback.

All the Best!

– Anatoly Volkhover

APPENDIX I
DEPENDENCY INVERSION EXPLAINED

> *There are nights when the wolves are silent and only the moon howls.*
>
> – *George Carlin*

Speaking with many software engineers, including very experienced ones, I realized that the purpose of Dependency Inversion is poorly or incorrectly understood. Many think of it as a "trick with interfaces" which somehow magically works. Let's demystify it.

Consider a highly hypothetical example. Imagine you quit your engineering career, and opened a pizza shop. Your main customer is a fast-growing high-tech startup down the street, which keeps you busy. The startup pays for the food, and they even streamlined their ordering by creating a Google Form for their employees. All an engineer has to do when they get hungry is fill in their name, select the desired toppings and push the Send button. This automatically emails the doc to you, and you make and deliver the pizza to the company's front desk. Easy.

Through the first year of your shop's existence, the startup expanded so much you were getting too many email orders to handle them manually. You dusted off your engineering skills, and wrote a little Python program, which parsed the incoming emails and entered the orders automatically into your point of sale system. This was possible because all emails shared the same consistent format, based on the same Google Form.

Another year passes, your business is thriving, and you go on a well-deserved vacation to Bora Bora. That's when an unimaginable happens. In an attempt to make the Google Form prettier, someone at the startup changes its format. The template now looks awesome, but the new format breaks your little Python automation. Your business immediately stalls, and you are too far away to fix it. Ouch!

Turns out that your business has a hidden *dependency*[43] on the form owned by your customer.

Sounds logical… but could you do better?

The answer is yes. You could provide your own form to the startup for ordering pizza. Heck, you could probably do better, and give them an online form. Either way, by publishing your own form, you could have *inverted* the dependency – making the startup employees dependent on your form, and not the other way around. All that was required from you is to clearly *declare the contract* for engaging your services.

In the nutshell, this is what *dependency inversion* is all about. It breaks the natural order in which the consumer of the data (the pizza shop) depends on the supplier of the data (the customer). It turns the tables, making the supplier dependent on the consumer.

We encounter Dependency Inversion every day, in our day to day life. Almost every time you are filling out a form to order a service, you are dealing with an inverted dependency. Service providers don't want to be dependent on you, and they invert the dependency by forcing you into compliance with their contracts (forms).

In software engineering, this is implemented through *interfaces*. An interface published by a service provider is an equivalent of the form handed out to a customer.

---

[43] When saying dependency, I mean the following: *A depends on B if changes made to B may require A to change*. In our example, a change to the ordering form by the startup (B) forces us (A) to rewrite our Python automation.

APPENDIX II
RECOMMENDED
READING MATERIALS

The reason I talk to myself is because I'm the only one whose answers I accept.

— George Carlin

Here are the books on the software architecture that will help you dig deeper into some of the topics brought up in this book:

- Clean Architecture, by Robert C. Martin

- Clean Code: A Handbook of Agile Software Craftsmanship, by Robert C. Martin

- Domain-Driven Design: Tackling Complexity in the Heart of Software, by Eric Evans

- CQRS (Command Query Responsibility Segregation), by Ajay Kumar

- Exploring CQRS and Event Sourcing (Microsoft patterns & practices), by Julian Dominguez, Grigori Melnik, Fernando Simonazzi, Mani Subramanian and Dominic Betts

- Design Patterns: Elements of Reusable Object-Oriented Software, by Erich Gamma, Richard Helm, Ralph Johnson and John Vlissides

- Object-Oriented Programming — The Trillion Dollar Disaster, by Ilya Suzdalnitski (published on Medium)

Made in the USA
Monee, IL
24 December 2023

50470308R00105